W. K. KELLOGG FUND

Growth Policy
Population, Environment, and Beyon

Kan Ch
Karl F. Lag

Mark R. B
E. Drannon Buskirk
Donald H. C
Karl Herpolshei
T. Jeffrey J
George
J. C. Ma
John McC
Donald N. Mi
Stephen M. Pc
Ruth R

Ann
The University of Michig

Grateful acknowledgment is made to the following publishers for permission to reprint copyrighted materials:

Baywood Publishing Company, Inc., for excerpts from Kan Chen, "A Macrosystem Analysis of the Human Environment." Reprinted by permission from the *Journal of Environmental Systems*.

The Conference Board, Inc., for an excerpt from Donald N. Michael, "The Individual: Enriched or Impoverished? Master or Servant?" Reprinted by permission from *Information Technology: Some Critical Implications for Decision Makers*.

Educational Technology Publications, Inc., for excerpts from Ronald G. Havelock, "Innovations in Education: Strategies and Tactics." Reprinted by permission from *The Change Agent's Guide to Innovation in Education*. Copyright © 1973 by Educational Technology Publications, Inc.

Little, Brown and Company, for a chart from John and Mildred Teal, *The Life and Death of the Salt Marsh*. Text, Copyright © 1969 by John and Mildred Teal. Reprinted by permission of Atlantic-Little, Brown and Co.

Quadrangle/The New York Times Book Co., for two figures from Eugene S. Schwartz, *Overskill: The Decline of Technology in Modern Civilization*. Copyright © 1971 by Eugene S. Schwartz. Reprinted by permission of Quadrangle/The New York Times Book Co.

The University of Wisconsin Press, for five figures from Robert F. Inger, Arthur D. Hasler, F. Herbert Bormann, and W. Frank Blair, eds., *Man in the Living Environment*. Copyright © 1972 by the Board of Regents of the University of Wisconsin. Reprinted by permission of The University of Wisconsin Press.

Preface

In the following study we attempt to be truly inter-disciplinary. We have integrated ideas and extensive contributions from persons in many disciplines into a coherent framework. At every stage, these persons interacted so that no chapter presents material from the exclusive perspective of any single discipline. This inter-disciplinary approach enabled us to be keenly appreciative of the subjectivity which exists in all policy research. We have not succumbed to the myth that policy research can be completely objective.

Rather than propose specific policies in this study, we undertake the task of determining how policy research could be done to enable policy makers to avoid the catastrophe that looms ahead for mankind if present trends of population growth and environmental impact continue. We attempt to strike a balance between substance, methodology, and process. With so many books and articles being published on the substance of the world problem we discuss, we think it appropriate to present a means of classifying these materials and to consider the policy-making process in depth, and then to integrate the two in a total systems approach methodology.

The resultant study can enlarge the public's appreciation of the nature of this macroproblem we face together and of the prerequisites for its solution. We hope, too, that the study can guide policy agencies and policy-influencing groups and stimulate them into comprehensive thinking about their plans for action. Finally, we see the study useful for advanced undergraduate students

89711

and for graduate students, especially those involved in interdisciplinary seminars in the relevant areas. They will appreciate, as we have learned to, the complexity of societal and environmental problems.

This book is one of the products of a National Science Foundation Planning Grant (No. GS-31522) to the University of Michigan for policy research on population and environment (Project PROPE). We were the coprincipal investigators of the research project. The resource for the project was augmented through the support of faculty time by the Paul G. Goebel Chair in Advanced Technology, College of Engineering, and by the Center for Population Planning at the University of Michigan.

We share coauthorship of this book with our colleagues: Donald H. Gray, associate professor of civil engineering; John McGuire, assistant professor of biostatistics and population planning; Donald N. Michael, professor of planning and public policy, professor of psychology, and program director at the Center for Research on Utilization of Scientific Knowledge; and Stephen M. Pollock, associate professor of industrial and operations engineering.

Sharing coauthorship, and responsible for integrating and editing the manuscript, was our colleague J. C. Mathes, associate professor of humanities, College of Engineering.

Also responsible for authorship are the following research associates: Mark R. Berg, mechanical engineering and urban and regional planning; E. Drannon Buskirk, Jr., biology and resource policy and administration; Karl Herpolsheimer, economics and finance; T. Jeffrey Jones, science engineering; George Kral, political science and urban planning; and Ruth Rehfus, library science and conservation.

Because this study is the product of the combined interdisciplinary efforts of so many persons, we are especially indebted to our executive secretary, Mrs. Hershall F. (Lois) Johnson, for her secretarial and administrative service. She was able to coordinate these many efforts through numerous stages to produce a finished manuscript far more polished than we could have hoped for.

We are also significantly indebted to Mrs. Suzanne Peang-Meth, research assistant, for her editorial, bibliographic, and secretarial contributions. A number of persons, inside and outside the University of Michigan, have given helpful counsel to our group. We would like to make the following special acknowledgments:

Robert W. Lamson, The National Science Foundation, provided the initial stimulation of our interdisciplinary effort in policy research on population and environment, introduced us to a number of policy agencies in the federal government, and furnished us a great deal of relevant reference materials.

Marc H. Ross, professor of physics at the University of Michigan, participated in and contributed to a number of technical discussions with us, especially related to the issues of economic growth and energy consumption.

George B. Simmons, assistant professor of economics and population planning at the University of Michigan, participated in many substantive discussions under Project PROPE especially related to economic and demographic models, and the international implications of growth policies.

Leslie Corsa, professor of public health and director of the Center for Population Planning at the University of Michigan, provided both substantive and administrative support for Project PROPE.

John R. Platt, associate director of the Mental Health Research Institute at the University of Michigan, has given us valuable advice regarding the relevant research being conducted at various "invisible colleges" and the possible directions for fruitful research.

Yuh-jao Wu, member of the Asian Ecology Group at the University of Michigan, made a significant contribution through his critique on the international issues discussed in chapter 7.

Duane S. Elgin, formerly on the staff of the Presidential Commission on Population Growth and the American Future, gave a special seminar in which the idea was first presented to us regarding the four interacting factors of population size, population distribution, resource consumption, and technology.

In addition, we developed many ideas as a result of special seminars given by:

O. Dudley Duncan, Charles Horton Cooley University Professor of Sociology, and associate director of the Population Studies Center at the University of Michigan, and commissioner, the Commission on Population Growth and the American Future

Ronald G. Ridker, Resources for the Future, Inc.

Joseph L. Sax, professor of law at the University of Michigan

Richard Sandler, formerly on U.S. Congressional staff

Furthermore, we have obtained valuable information and advice during our interviews with a number of persons, including Joan Hock, Council on Environmental Quality; George Brosseau, The National Science Foundation; Martin Prochnik, U.S. Department of the Interior; Allen Kneese, Resources for the Future, Inc.; Richard Balzhiser, U.S. Office of Science and Technology; Sara Mazie, Commission on Population Growth and the American Future; William Van Ness, Senate Committee on Interior and Insular Affairs; and Daniel Dreyfus, Senate Committee on Interior and Insular Affairs.

Further advice came from interviews with Wallace D. Bowman, Library of Congress; Carl Pope, Zero Population Growth; Jeannie Rosoff, Planned Parenthood-World Population; Carl Schultz, Office of Population Affairs, U.S. Department of Health, Education and Welfare; Phillip Friedly, U.S. Department of Housing and Urban Development; Charles Leppert, House Committee on Interior and Insular Affairs; Helen Wilson, Applied Urbanetics, Inc.; and Jonathan Brown, aide to Congressman Marvin Esch, as well as other congressional staff members too numerous to mention.

Assistance in the global context was provided by Dr. Adeke Boerma, director general, Food and Agricultural Organization (FAO) Rome; Mr. Ralph Townley, United Nations Development Programme (UNDP), New York; the World Health Organization (WHO); The Club of Rome; Battelle; and the Agency for International Development (AID).

Many units of the University of Michigan cooperated to expedite our effort:

The Institute for Environmental Quality
The Institute for Social Research
The Office of Research Administration
The School of Natural Resources
The College of Engineering

Among the many helpful individuals at the University were:

A. Geoffrey Norman, vice-president for Research
Gordon J. Van Wylen, dean, College of Engineering
James McFadden, dean, School of Natural Resources
James T. Wilson, director, Institute of Science and Technology

We are very grateful to all of the foregoing and to others, some of whom are variously acknowledged in the text, for their assistance, kindness, and understanding.

KAN CHEN

KARL F. LAGLER

Contents

Growth Policy

Chapter I

Growth Policy: Beyond the Present

The *Seventh Seal* of Ingmar Bergman opens as the knight, Antonius Block, returns to Sweden after a ten-year crusade to the Holy Land. The plague rages throughout the land. Before he can reach his home, Antonius Block meets Death; however, he arranges with Death for a reprieve while the two play a game of chess. Their game continues throughout the film, and Antonius Block is able to avoid defeat long enough for him to reach his wife. He has a brief moment of reunion with her before Death gathers them in. With the reprieve, he has achieved more than this reunion. By playing the chess game effectively enough to prolong the end, he enables a young couple, Jof and Mia, and their child to escape Death for the present and to anticipate a natural life cycle. This family greets the sunrise with hope, and the human community continues.

Man today faces an analogous situation. A plague may be imminent, but a plague that cannot be cured through faith, technology, or perseverance alone or severally because it has global dimensions, many unknown complications, and a dynamic behavior difficult to anticipate. We refer to this plague as the *macroproblem* caused by the accelerating growth of population, technological development, and consumption that even now places unprecedented pressure on the earth's natural resources, environmental systems, and human cultures. This macro-problem could be so catastrophic as to render insignificant all previous plagues, earthquakes, tidal waves, and wars combined that the human race has endured. One extrapolation (Forrester, 1971, p. 81), though admittedly controversial, is that from 2030 to 2060 the world population could fall from about six billion persons to slightly less than one billion persons, with a death rate rising during that time to a maximum near 400 million persons per year.

The expansion of human activity has been characterized by exponential population growth, increasing density (urbanization) of the population, acceleration of economic output and resource consumption, and massive technological intervention in diverse natural systems. The impact of this growth is described by the concept of ecological demand (SCEP, 1970, pp. 118–20), which aggregates the utilization of resources and the disposal of wastes, and more importantly which recognizes that the total impact of human activity is greater than the sum of individual actions, such as the effects of specific pollutants or depletions of specific resources. The totality of this impact results from basic synergisms inherent in all complex ecological systems. Because of an extensive web of linkages (E. P. Odum, 1969), each human activity affects many components of the energy and material flows in an ecosystem. In addition, man's goal of enhancing the productivity of the overall ecosystem that supports him, the Earth or "the ecosphere," is achieved at the expense of ecosystem diversity and stability (H. T. Odum, 1971), although these features apparently are necessary for its survival. Other impacts of human activity on the natural system that sustains him include climatic changes, geophysical changes, redistributions or eliminations of plant and animal species, introduction of foreign substances toxic to the system, and of mutagenic agents of uncertain effects.

The impact of man on the ecosphere suggests that growth of human activity must be controlled by recognition of ecosystem parameters and acceptance of ecosystem constraints if man and other living elements of the system are to survive. Controlling the growth and impact will be difficult. The human system has shown itself unable to adjust toward an equilibrium with its environment (for a discussion of homeostasis in social systems, see Caldwell, 1969). The task we set for ourselves is to suggest a policy-making approach that could enable the human system to adjust to this new situation. We believe policy makers henceforth must directly consider problems associated with population growth and the consequent impact on the environment if their many particular policy decisions are to avoid deleterious effects.

We recognize that some persons will view this effort as unnecessary. They will react to our references to the *Seventh Seal* and to Jay Forrester's prognostications in *World Dynamics* as alarmist and unfounded. They will assert that the ingredients of the problems have existed throughout human history, and that mankind somehow has survived and even prospered. Finally, they will assert that man's ingenuity and his marvelous science and technology will enable him to overcome these problems and indeed the macroproblem.

These persons have, we think, a Crystal Palace syndrome. At the Great London Exhibition of the Works of Industry of All Nations in 1851, the Crystal Palace, an innovative architectural integration of glass and iron symbolized to almost everyone the radiant future the human mind and technology would create as civilization progressed. The true visionary, however, may have been Fyo-dor Dostoevsky, who traveled to see the Crystal Palace and marveled at this "colossal idea" amidst "that polluted Thames, that air saturated with coal dust; . . . those terrible sections of the city like Whitechapel with its half-naked, savage, and hungry population" (Dostoevsky, 1863, p. 90). Although the Thames itself has been improved, the London of 1860 could well be the world Forrester projects. Local short-run solutions, especially the technological ones favored by policy makers, no longer suffice.

What has become increasingly evident in the century since Dostoevsky ironically commented on the blessings of a technological society is the need to redefine the premises and the philosophic foundations of technology (Mathes, 1971), and to challenge effectively the growth ethic of Western civilization.

For the first time in history man may not be able to overcome the macroproblem mainly through technology, for technology up to now has been able to wield its power primarily by bleeding natural resources and the environment (Chen, 1971). An increasing number of persons, including scientists, suggest we are approaching the ultimate limits of resource use and environmental manipulation faster than most people realize. Given the very long time constants in the macroproblem—the time it requires for a population to stabilize, for certain irreversible environmental impacts to be widely recognized, and for our social and political institutions to make fundamental policy changes—civilization may soon become unable to avert the dire consequences of the world macroproblem. But if we begin now, there still may be time to devise solutions.

In this study we do not wish to debate the issue of whether or not the macroproblem exists. That issue is and will continue to be debated in many arenas. We think it just as appropriate to make the assumption that the macroproblem *could* exist. All of us should agree that the one thing known on this issue is that no one at present knows for certain what the future holds. Rather than debate the macroproblem, we assume its existence so that we can go on to explore methods of coping with it. Certainly the long time constants and the complexity of the macroproblem justify making that assumption now. By the time the existence of the macroproblem would be accepted and the form of the macroproblem would be understood by all, it would be too late to formulate and then implement policies that could deal with it.

The moment seems propitious for making such an assumption. The United States as a nation appears to be ready at the policy level to consider the existence of a world macroproblem. A great deal of public pressure and crusading spirit to restore our environment has been generated in the last five years (Chen, 1971, p. 135). These have helped encourage the federal government to establish the Presidential Council on Environmental Quality, the Environmental Protection Agency, and the Commission on Population Growth and the American Future, which issued its final report in March, 1972. In addition, many state and local governments have established counterparts of these agencies. Furthermore, because environmental problems recognize no national boundaries, worldwide concern on environmental issues has gathered a great deal of momentum, as evidenced by the discussions surrounding the United Nations Conference on the Human Environment at Stockholm in June, 1972.

Although the number of publications and agencies dealing with the macroproblem in one way or another already is voluminous, and continues to increase, we would be greatly amiss to identify with these activities a corresponding rate of effective solutions to the macroproblem. If we try to distill meaningful concerted actions from the heated debates on population and environmental issues, we can find few action-oriented policies that are generally acceptable and that measure up to the magnitude of the macroproblem. Although a number of future-oriented thinkers have taken global views of population and environmental issues, they tend to represent their respective professions or disciplines. Their views frequently are charged with emotions or prejudicial values and have not been integrated with actual policy-making processes or with assessment procedures for determining progress in solving the macroproblem.

We have two particular concerns in this study. Although for the first time man may have the means to control his future, we do not think present policy-making approaches allow for effective analysis of the macroproblem, and we do not think that present decision-making contexts and procedures can yield adequate solutions to the macroproblem. Suppose that Antonius Block had approached his chess game with Death as present policy makers approach problems. In this case, Antonius Block would not have concerned himself with long-range strategy and with the overall dimensions of the chess game. He instead would have concentrated on capturing one of Death's pawns posing an immediate threat to one of his own bishops. Devising his tactics to capture the pawn would have rendered him fatally vulnerable several moves hence, and his king would have been checkmated. With this approach, then, Antonius Block would not have been reunited with his wife, even briefly. With this approach Jof and Mia and their child would not have escaped to make the future of mankind possible. The person who cannot coordinate and anticipate the moves of all of his pieces far into the future of the game is defeated before he has a chance to make many moves at all.

We think man must begin to play the game in earnest. We do not know whether or not he can avert catastrophe. But we do know that if the macroproblem, even in part, actually threatens us we have no chance unless we coordinate our activities and anticipate future impacts. Before we can do these we must: appreciate the pervasive nature of the macroproblem; accept the very high degree of uncertainty in both the physical and the behavioral aspects of the systems involved; and recognize the polemic value implications underlying policy issues. Therefore, rather than delve substantively into specific policy research areas, we endeavor to establish meaningful guidelines and procedures for concerned persons to consider and for future policy research on population and the environment. Our emphases are: (1) to provide an overall framework to put in proper perspective the vast amount of results and ideas that have been and will be generated elsewhere; and (2) to establish the criteria for coupling future policy research on the macroproblem to policy-making procedures.

Establishing a perspective commensurate with the scope of the macroproblem leads us to challenge the growth ethic and the assumptions behind it, and to redefine what is meant by the term "growth." Until we perceive the problem in a way it has not been perceived up to now, we cannot identify and evaluate a sufficiently wide range of possible policies for dealing with the macroproblem. To generate these policies we propose a comprehensive policy-making procedure, a systems approach commensurate with the dynamics and the complexity of the total ecosystem of the earth (which we define to include the human sphere). This synoptic procedure leads us to challenge the conventional wisdom and assumptions behind current policy making, which is a disjointed incremental process inadequate for the magnitude and complexity of the macroproblem. Such a challenge of current policy making leads us to question the ability of present political and policy-making institutions to cope with the macroproblem. These institutions, of course, are not inherently bad, and have served us fairly well up to the present. The sudden emergence of the macroproblem as a concept to consider seriously, however, indicates that in essence the reality of the situation has changed, and that consequently present institutions have become inappropriate. Our assessment furthermore leads us to anticipate a change from the elitism inherent in present policy-making procedures to an inclusion of many segments of the population in the policy-making process in an increasingly participatory manner. Pervading our entire analysis of the policy-making process and the policy-making environment is a recognition of their inherent subjectivity—subjectivity which must be made explicit, accepted, and dealt with rationally if one is to approach the macroproblem effectively.

Because of its complexity and the cultural differences as to values, priorities, and levels of economic development, the macroproblem continues to be poorly defined in spite of accepted recognition of its four basic causative factors: (1) population growth; (2) population distribution; (3) resource consumption; and (4) technological development. Further definition and articulation of the world macroproblem is a prerequisite for future attempts to develop a common view of reality and a corresponding macropolicy. Once the macroproblem is defined, the vacuum of long-range policies can be filled and man's disruptions of the ecosphere reduced only if we generate and implement policies aimed at carefully chosen futures rather than at possibilities determined by traditional values and perspectives incompatible with solutions to the macroproblem.

To set the stage for this definition, in accordance with an ecosystem perspective, we outline schemes for classifying environmental impacts and policy responses. Ecosystemic classification uncovers many ecosystem linkages affected by human activity but not usually considered by policy makers. Methodologies are needed to assess the impacts on these linkages of population growth, population distribution, resource consumption, and technological development. The classification of policies by these four policy types enables us to challenge the basic assumptions of current policies and to devise a method of widening policy alternatives within each of the four categories and particularly by carefully chosen combinations from the policy types.

These four areas of human activity create environmental problems which demand new modes of policy responses consistent with the integrity of the ecosystem. First, policy on population size cannot be considered in isolation from population distribution, resource consumption, and technology. In this context, policy on population size has to go beyond family planning activities to consider measures to reduce the number of births desired, as well as encourage research into social, cultural, and environmental factors that affect fertility. Second, population distribution patterns no longer should be allowed to develop free from purposeful policy controls. Policy planning in this area, especially that related to urbanization, must consider the synergistic interaction of population, resource consumption, and technological and economic variables. Particularly pernicious in this regard is the current assumption that socioeconomic problems and environmental problems are separate. Since efficient exploitation of the environment is related to the manner in which population is distributed, decentralized population distribution patterns must be established as viable policy alternatives.

Third, current policy on resource consumption is anchored on prevailing economic beliefs. However, internalization of externalities, the economic approach to environmental problems, does not affect the basic forces behind growth. From an ecosystem perspective, an alternative approach would be to consider the *stock* of resources (Boulding, 1966) more important than resource consumption, or *flow* of resources. This leads to serious consideration of a stationary-state economy and, consequently, of specific criteria for a successful challenge of the growth ethic and of the prevailing image of progress.

Fourth, present policy makers look to technology to relax ecosystem constraints rather than to curb rates of growth and consumption. Consequently, technological development exacerbates the macroproblem. Technological "solutions" generate residue problems that proliferate faster than problems are solved. Even the most well-intentioned technological projects often have unanticipated and highly disruptive ecological impacts (for instances, Farvar and Milton, 1972). We must, therefore, create a new concept of technological "progress." In addition, we need a rational ecosystem approach to technology assessment that will account for related population and consumption demands.

Finally, taken together, these four policy categories yield a major premise of our study. A policy response to a particular socioenvironmental problem cannot be restricted to a single policy type and, in turn, cannot be developed with a disjointed incremental approach to policy making. An assortment of policy alternatives provided by a macrosystems approach to policy planning enables truly flexible responses to system stresses and thus contributes to ecosystem stability, and consequently to our very survival.

A systems approach is needed to manage the macroproblem because of the dynamic nature of the macroproblem (i.e., the rates of change) and the complexity of component interactions. This approach requires the use of at least one important technique of systems analysts—mathematical modeling. Present economic, demographic, and environmental models are relatively insensitive to the ecosystemic uncertainties associated with their component variables. Despite acknowledged deficiencies (e.g., static time periods), models can provide insights into system interactions, and should be used to aid in the selection of policy alternatives. The tradeoffs between benefits and risks can be studied by decision analysis techniques. Other evaluation techniques, as well as means of identifying values underlying environmental tradeoffs, can be developed.

Our analysis of the macroproblem relies on a comprehensive systems approach to policy research which we develop from systems analysis methodologies. As mentioned above, we predicate our systems approach on an explicit recognition of the subjectivity underlying the entire process. Subjectivity in this sense is explored by Kenneth Boulding in his book *The Image,* and is inherent in individual and collective perceptions of empirical reality as well as of needs and values. The basic issues underlying decision making have their source in differences between our perceptions or images.

Once this subjectivity is recognized, the policy maker generates a wide range of alternative policies based on a synoptic image of reality which includes all possible impacts as well as all possible interactions of the four dynamic variables—population size, population distribution, resource consumption, and technology. We put this systems approach into an operational framework consisting of three stages: (1) a comprehensive view for understanding, involving identification of basic issues and the ecosystem classification scheme discussed above; (2) an expanded look at specific policies and impacts, enabling us to identify the specific policy research needs; and (3) an overview for actual policy decision. In the comprehensive overview stage we relate policy research to policy making, and especially to the policy-making environment.

The macrosystems approach cannot become operative until the policy-making environment changes significantly. The present policy-making process, characterized by disjointed incrementalism, has developed because of very real constraints of men and organizations. Currently, the many uncertainties and alternatives, combined with the rational limitations of the individual human mind, lead policy makers to consider policies that differ only incrementally from existing policies. In addition, ends are chosen primarily because they are appropriate for the means available, and these ends usually are negative in the sense that they attempt to correct ills rather than implement objectives (Lindblom, 1965, pp. 215–16).

In such an environment the policy maker concerns himself with parochial interests rather than the interests of society in general. The welfare of society is assumed to be served by the combined actions of numerous separate individual policy decisions. If problems are ignored in one policy-making arena, they are assumed to be addressed in another.

These assumptions are not adequate for a macro-problem situation. No problem is isolated in its definition and solution; furthermore, events interact over time and require policy-making procedures to be continually adjusted to these changes. This requires goal setting and evaluation of the performance of the actions initiated by policy decisions. The setting of goals and values needs to involve all segments of the population affected, and needs as well to transcend the pressing realities of the moment. Future-responsive policies designed for implementation in the present will be crucial for long-range social and ecosystem welfare.

The type of policy research needed for synoptic policy making is now seldom done and is essentially unused. Nor will the research or the synoptic policy making be done until policy makers and policy-making institutions respond to social pressures for them to take a comprehensive approach. When these pressures become intense, unprecedented opportunities for synoptic policy making in the domain of the macroproblem will be created. When this occurs, policy research comparable to that we propose in this study and policy procedures similar to those we delineate must be available. In anticipation of the future opportunities for synoptic policy making we develop the macrosystems approach in the following chapter.

Chapter II

The Macrosystems Approach and Policy Judgment on Growth

We have initially explained how the interacting growths of population, the economy, and technology create a macroproblem that cannot be approached with present policy-making processes. To find effective solutions to the macroproblem, new policy-making processes must be developed. In a fundamental way, the disjointed incrementalism of the present policy-making process is at best incongruent with the solution and at worst contributes to the forces causing the macroproblem. The ingredients of the macroproblem are highly interactive and their dynamics have very long time constants. Thus, the piecemeal approach of generating and implementing policy decisions in a disjointed incremental manner is antithetical to the long-range ecosystem approach required by the macroproblem.

If the disjointed incremental characteristics of the policy-making process were to remain unchanged, much of our study as well as most policy research on the macroproblem would be futile. There are encouraging signs, however, that our increasingly turbulent society will become more amenable to new policy-making processes. The systems framework and procedures for future policy research we present are based on the assumption that this change in the policy-making environment indeed will occur. The forces underlying this change will mutually reinforce an expansion of the systems approach to policy research and lead to comprehensive or synoptic policy making.

A Macrosystems Approach

Systems analysis as developed by engineers for large-scale physical systems development (typified by examples of aerospace projects) and by economists for rational resource allocation related to multiagency programs (typified by examples in defense planning) serves as a point of departure to develop a comprehensive systems approach to policy research. Heretofore, the application of systems analysis methodologies to various social problems has been only partially successful because policy research for social policy making is inherently value-laden in all its aspects, from determination of which problems to solve first to inclusion of specific values in particular solutions. Policy makers must make this subjectivity explicit in order to deal with it properly. In addition, they must acknowledge the divergent value systems in a pluralistic society. Until they do these, the results of policy research will only add confusion to controversies in public debate or serve the purpose of a single participant group in the play of power (Lindblom, 1968).

If the policy researcher recognizes this subjectivity, he can play the useful role of illuminator, arbitrator, and change agent. Consequently, we predicate our systems approach on an explicit delineation of this subjectivity. To do this, we expand on the usual function of the systems analyst in policy research. Then we discuss the analysis of basic issues, values, and judgmental procedures.

The usual professional function of the systems analyst in policy research is to map alternative policies to

their corresponding impacts or effects. In terms of mathematical concepts, he is to "map the policy space" (which
contains all possible combinations of policies) "into the
impact space" (which has the dimension of all significant
impact variables). This mapping operation is conceptually
displayed in figure 1.

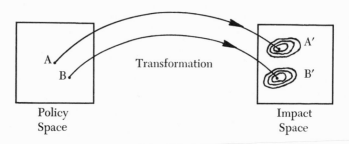

Fig. 1. Mapping of relationships, the conventional function of
the systems analyst.

The arrows indicate the transformation frequently
represented by a mathematical function. Thus from policy A, transformation would identify impact (outcome)
A'. Concentric contours in the impact space represent
confidence intervals; that is, they symbolize that transformations of social policies usually are not deterministic,
and contain uncertainties or probabilities. The unidirec-
tional arrows in figure 1 represent only one part of the
thinking process, the part to which the conventional systems analyst primarily contributes. The other part of the
thinking process concerns the generation of policy options.

Although the systems approach to policy research as
represented in figure 1 is a very broad concept, it brings
forth only some of the elements of subjectivity embedded
in the process. For example, the choice between policy A
and policy B can be made partly by evaluating their re-

spective impacts. Which impact is better would be judged according to specified subjective criteria. Another subjective element is represented by the concentric contours in figure 1. These result from uncertainties in the parameters of the transformation, and these uncertainties may be encoded in terms of subjective probabilities obtained from expert judgment.

Several important elements of subjectivity, however, are not evident in figure 1. The very structure of the transformation, not just its parameters, is subjective because it represents the reality image (world view) of the analyst. Depending on his image of the impact space, he includes certain variables or dimensions (e.g., immediate and quantifiable costs and benefits), and excludes others (e.g., long-term ecological balance). Sometimes the analyst recognizes the importance of certain impact variables, but the lack of undisputed transformation from the policy space to the impact space spanned by these variables leads him to make the expedient choice of ignoring them. For example, consider the value implications of a specific policy to liberalize abortion laws. The primary impact of legal abortion on population size can be assessed relatively easily from historical evidence. The secondary impacts on social values and conducts, however, such as respect for life, violence, and responsible sexual behavior, have been quite controversial. To bring forth these secondary impacts considered in real decision making, the systems approach in policy research must be expanded as conceptually displayed in figure 2.

The subjectivity can now be made explicit. When left implicit, it often restricts policy makers to a very limited domain of "practical considerations" within the potential policy space. Wider considerations often are tabooed by traditional values or beyond the fields of

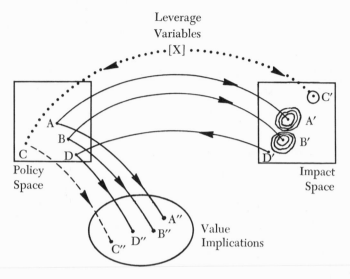

Fig. 2. The element of subjectivity added to conventional systems analysis.

traditional reality images. Yet the primary purpose of policy research is to generate a wide range of alternative policies in order to examine many different specific possible policies. To do this, policy research must stimulate unconventional thinking.

The conventional approach is to begin from the policy space. The figure suggests alternatives, however. For example, we could begin from a desirable point in the impact space and try to locate the "inverse image" in the policy space. Rather than ask what policies are available and where they will lead, we could ask where we want to be and determine what policies would move society in that direction. Then the value implications of the policies would be determined, as illustrated by D, D′ and D″ in figure 2, and, considering the desirable primary impact, the desirable policy chosen. This inverse transformation some-times is difficult to perform, so another approach would be to begin with the leverage variables which act be-tween the policy space and the impact space. These are symbolically represented by the symbol [X] and the bro-ken curves linking C, C' and C'' in figure 2. We focus on leverage variables in our policy research on the macro-problem because policy decisions effect different out-comes in the impact space according to how the decisions alter the relevant leverage variables—population size and distribution, resource consumption, and technological development.

To help us think about policy research in this area, we ask these fundamental questions (paraphrased from Lamson, 1969):

1. What would be the impacts of alternative patterns of population and techno-economic growths on natu-ral resources, the environment, and the total ecosys-tem including man and society?

2. What are the policies that would be required to reach the alternative goals of population and tech-no-economic growths?

In terms of figure 2, we start by focusing on the leverage variables, and then proceed to the impact and policy spaces.

To seek specific answers to these questions, we would follow the logical steps in the procedural frame-work illustrated in figure 3. These steps (Chen, 1971, pp. 147–49) are:

1. Select population and techno-economic variables ([X] in figure 2)

2. Make assumptions about the variables

3. Make projections of the variables

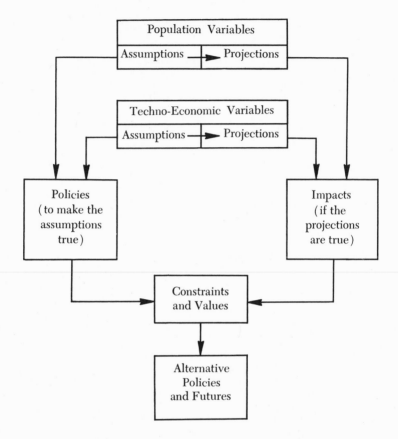

Fig. 3. Procedure for policy research on macroproblem
(adapted from Chen, 1971, p. 146).

4. Specify impacts (determine C′ in figure 2)
5. Specify policies (determine C in figure 2)
6. Analyze constraints, alternative goals, and values
(determine C″ and compare with C′ in figure 2)
7. Outline alternative policies and alternative futures
(list A, B, C, D along with A′, B′, C′, D′ and A″, B″,
C″, D″ in figure 2)

1. Select population and techno-economic variables ([X] in figure 2)

Since population growth and techno-economic growth are considered as the primary forces which have exerted pressure on all aspects of the human and natural environment, we select leverage variables that quantitatively describe these primary forces of growth. For example, the population size leverage variable would be described by lower-level variables such as the rates of birth, death, immigration, and emigration. The variables describing the techno-economic leverage variable would include the GNP derived from both the production of goods and services because their technologies and productions have different effects on the environment (e.g., different generations of waste products). It will also be important to select a variable which reflects the per capita GNP gap between the well-developed and the less-developed countries. The less-developed countries, which have a majority of the earth's population, are striving to narrow this gap. Their success or failure will have a profound impact on the global environment.

2. Make assumptions about the variables

Since the objective of policy research is to identify alternative policies and relate them to alternative futures, a *range* of assumptions would be made for the selected population and techno-economic variables. The range would include the current growth trends, their reasonable variations, and some drastic changes that have been proposed seriously.

3. Make projections of the variables

Based on each set of assumptions, projections would be made on population and techno-economic growth patterns. For example, population growth projections would be made in terms of the age structure and would relate to a leverage variable we separate out for discussion in the next chapter, population distribution. Techno-economic growth projections would be made in terms of energy consumption, demand for raw materials, etc., based on assumed and projected factors of production. Maximum use would be made of existing projections and information. However, existing projections tend to begin with a given set, rather than a range, of assumptions. Therefore, our approach would encourage the expansion of existing projections in order to aid policy decision making.

4. Specify impacts (determine C' in figure 2)

The impacts on the environment would be specified for each set of projections of population and techno-economic growth patterns. The impacts to be specified in directions and in magnitude would include the kinds and amounts of wastes produced, the impact on resource consumption (land, food, minerals, energy, etc.), and the demand on our service systems (education, housing, transport, communications, etc.).

5. Specify policies (determine C in figure 2)

The policies required to realize the various assumptions would be specified next. For example, the requirements to realize certain population growth patterns could be analyzed in terms of the average number of children wanted and the cost and availability of family planning assistance. The requirements to bring about certain techno-economic growth patterns would include some minimum increase of productivity and of capital cumulation rate, along with various technological developments.

6. Analyze constraints, alternative goals, and values (determine C" and compare with those of C' in figure 2)

Solutions to problems caused by the impacts of population and techno-economic growth on the environment are relative. The pressures of this growth could be reduced either by curtailing growth or by generating resources, the latter including new technologies for resource exploitation.

7. Outline alternative policies and alternative futures (list A, B, C, D along with A', B', C', D' and A'', B'', C'', D'' in figure 2)

Based on the alternative goals obtained from step 6, alternative policies for reaching these goals would be outlined. The alternative policies would act in the domains of population size, population distribution, resource consumption, or technology, and probably would involve selected policy mixes from these domains. The long-term effects of these policies also would be assessed. For example, the policy of circumventing certain constraints in the near future might lead to more traumatic pressures and perhaps a greater collapse in the more distant future. For each set of alternative policies, the corresponding alternative future would be described in terms of its growth pattern, the environmental impacts, and the value implications of the pattern and corresponding policies.

The procedures in figure 3 serve as a useful initial framework for a systems approach to that aspect of policy research which generates and evaluates policy alternatives. To develop the macrosystems approach to an operational level, however, this framework needs to be expanded. In order to perceive and define constraints, goals, and values, we need to develop methods for understanding and resolving the basic issues inherent in the macroproblem. In order to define impacts, policies, and variables, we need to establish an ecosystem perspective. And, most important, to propose a transition to synoptic policy making on national and global levels we need to identify the requisite professional skills and institutional arrangements. To accomplish these will require policy researchers, policy makers, and policy constituencies to assess and readjust some of their fundamental images of the world and of man's role on earth.

As a start toward readjustment, we develop an operational framework for the policy research procedure itemized above. This framework, figure 4, describes the macrosystems approach we present in the following chapters.

The operational framework includes three major stages: a comprehensive view for understanding, an expanded look at specific policies and impacts, and an overview for action. These three stages are interconnected by communication and feedback channels that for the sake of clarity are not displayed explicitly. The comprehensive view is an image comprehending the scope of the macroproblem. Since policy considerations at this level can become vague, specific policies and impacts have to be focused upon in order to generate detailed policy alternatives. These alternatives become too narrowly conceived, however, unless they in turn are brought up to the level of an overview for action. The steps we follow within the operational framework are briefly explained below, and then in following chapters are explained in more detail with some illustrative examples. The steps within the operational framework are:

1. Identification of the basic issues
2. Classification of policies and impacts
3. Expansion and deliberation on the policy menu
4. Comparison of policies with respect to impacts
5. Outline of alternative policies and alternative futures

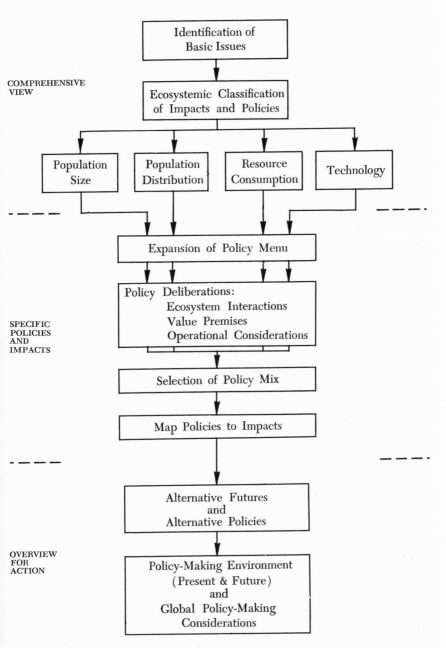

Fig. 4. An operational framework for policy research procedure to study population and the environment.

6. Considerations of the policy-making environments and the international interdependency of policy making.

1. *Identification of the basic issues*

The basic issues underlying the macroproblem are associated with challenges to the "growth ethic," which has deemed it good to have ever more people and more consumption of goods. To understand the basic issues, we must uncover the many conflicting images and assumptions hidden beneath the actual policy controversies. This requires an understanding of three kinds of interacting subjective judgments—reality, value, and instrumental. These judgments reflect our empirical and normative perceptions of the world. The controversies over the efficacy of growth as a social policy therefore result from different images of the impact of growth on man and the ecosystem. We must challenge and assess these images in order to develop a critical stance which can be used to map a wider range of alternative policies to alternative futures. Such a stance is for methodological purposes only. We do not take an advocacy position for any of the alternative policies. Instead, we are concerned with development of a macrosystem methodology able to transcend the parochial perspectives of current images.

2. *Classification of policies and impacts*

There are a number of ways of classifying policies and impacts. Rather than start from perspectives associated with the traditional growth ethic, we use an eco-system scheme to classify impacts. This scheme classifies impacts in four spheres: the atmosphere, the hydrosphere, the lithosphere, and the biosphere—which to us includes the hominisphere (the sphere of the man). The interfaces between the hominisphere and the rest of the ecosphere then are illuminated by a division of the hominisphere in terms of four dynamic factors: population size, population distribution, resource consumption, and technology.* These four are what we consider primary leverage variables, identified in figure 2 by the symbol [X]. The leverage variables are used to classify policies within the ecosystem scheme.

3. Expansion and deliberation on the policy menu

On the basis of the enlarged perspectives created in steps 1 and 2, we can expand the policy menu; that is, we can expand the range of possible policy choices. By challenging the core assumptions of prevailing policies in each category identified by a leverage variable, we can generate these additional specific policy possibilities. These new policies then can be compared and evaluated in terms of their ecosystem impacts and interactions, value premises, and instrumental considerations such as technological feasibility and economic viability. Traditional policy evaluation has been limited to short-term instrumental considerations. A comprehensive policy research approach considerably widens and lengthens the perspective on policy.

4. Comparison of policies with respect to impacts

After a wide range of alternative policies is generated, the potential impacts of specific policies need to be determined. This process of mapping policies to impacts can be greatly facilitated by the use of analytical models because reality judgments are involved in mapping poli-

---

° We are indebted to Duane Elgin [1971] for our analysis of the leverage variables in terms of these four factors. He discussed the synergic interaction of these in a working paper prepared for the Commission on Population Growth and the American Future.

cies to impacts, especially very long-term impacts. Analytical models, being the explications of mental images, can make explicit these controversial subjective structures and parameters. Used to clarify the differences between mental images, analytical models aid research and experimentation programs to shed light on the macroproblem as well as to provide social learning tools (Dunn, 1971). Models traditionally operate on the instrumental level; we propose that one be developed to operate on the level of the comprehensive overview for action.

5. *Outline of alternative policies and alternative futures*

At this step, we enlarge our perspective to that of a comprehensive overview of policy planning. The choice of any combination of specific policies with respect to the macroproblem implies acceptance of certain basic assumptions and social values, which define the kind of society people want. To help public debate and policy decision, it is useful to outline the alternative futures in terms of their growth patterns, the corresponding ecosystem impacts, the policy alterations required to reach the alternative futures, and the value changes that must accompany the growth patterns and the corresponding policies. The broad tradeoffs between ecosystem risks, preservation of traditional values, and changes of life styles can be made only at this overview level.

6. *Considerations of the policy-making environment and the international interdependency of policy making*

The steps described above can not yet lead to the selection of specific policies. Selection remains the prerogative of the policy makers and in turn of the public, acting through the political process. This systems approach, however, does assume that the policy makers or the users of policy research will be receptive to synoptic policy making and thus will see a use for the macrosystem approach. Furthermore, the approach as described assumes that the policy makers or the users of policy research will become involved in the research process, or at least be very accessible to the researchers. This is necessary because the steps described contain many elements of subjectivity, and because the researcher must take a critical stance. Yet to serve its intended purpose, the approach requires an intimate relationship and a mutual confidence between the user and the researcher.

Finally, the approach suggests a long and continuing process of joint learning and mutual support between the user and the researcher. If the results of policy research actually are to be used, both the user and the researcher must anticipate this need and build up a long-term working relationship. Nothing can be more erroneous than if the framework in figure 4 were to be taken as a once-through procedure for arriving at definitive solutions to the macroproblem within a limited time. The systems approach by definition assumes continuous feedback and monitoring, and consequently continued redefinition of goals.

The policy-making environment therefore must be considered in any policy-making procedure. At the macroproblem level, however, this policy-making environment must be enlarged to include the global environment within which United States policy decisions on population and the environment must be made.

The macroproblem is of worldwide significance, so no country, including the United States, can afford to set its growth policy parochially. In the absence of an effective supranational organization for potential conflict resolution or global policy making, United States growth policy must be considered on an interdependent basis along with the growth policies of other nations or nation blocs. Like those in many other complex international strategy situations, the interdependent decisions can be analyzed from a number of positions—rational, organizational, and political. In the final analysis, however, life on earth can survive only if all nations give due consideration to our common future as fellow human beings. At the conclusion of this study, therefore, we find it desirable for the United States to encourage such considerations in the formulation of policy decisions.

Basic Issues: The Challenge to Growth and Policy Judgments

As we have explained, the accelerating growth of population, technology, and the economy place unprecedented pressure on the world ecosystem. A solution to this macroproblem will require all peoples, and especially those associated with policy making, to challenge and reassess their fundamental images of reality and values in order to comprehend the implications of the consequent change. In terms of order of magnitude of the changes during the past century alone, John Platt (Platt, 1969, p. 1115) estimates increases of 10^7 in communication speed; 10^2 in travel speeds; 10^6 in data handling speeds; 10^3 in energy resources; 10^6 in power of weapons; and 10^2 in disease control. To these can be added for the United States increases in GNP of a factor of 18 (Kuznets, 1971, p. 6) and in population of a factor of 4. The magnitude and impacts of this growth still are difficult to comprehend, although advocates of growth are convinced that these increases have brought tremendous benefits. Perhaps the most serious challenge that policy planners must heed, and one increasingly heard in this nation, is the challenge to the "growth ethic." This challenge asserts that the long-term stability of the ecosystem and the survival of man are not compatible with the growth ethic and its implicit philosophy of "more." Man, as other elements in the ecosystem, has matured to the point where he must begin the difficult transition to a steady state (Daly, 1971) and its implicit philosophy of "enough" (Looft, 1971).

The impacts of exponential growth are explored in literature in the fields of population, economics, science and technology, communications, agriculture, education, armaments, transportation, natural resources, energy, etc. Concern over these impacts leads to a challenge to growth, which basically is a challenge of a fundamental American goal as well as a primary goal of many of the developing nations. Called into question are traditional methods of coping with the environmental and resource constraints imposed on man by the ecosystem. Few today would argue that pressures on these constraints are not approaching critical levels. The basic issue is: How should these pressures be reduced? Should we, as in the past two centuries, reduce them by pushing back the constraints through the techno-economic solutions associated with the growth ethic? Or should we accept these constraints by rejecting the growth ethic? A third option is to redefine our basic images and achieve a synthesis of the other two options.

The controversy over whether to continue to embrace or to reject the growth ethic is the form in which the issue is usually debated. For example, in the area of population the options posed are: Should we allow overall population levels to be determined by individuals, relatively insulated from public policy, and then attempt to reduce the environmental pressure through changes in

agriculture, new towns, new institutions, etc.? Or should
we reduce the source of the pressure by attempting to influence and reduce overall population levels? In the area
of resource consumption the options posed are: Should
we use economic adjustments and the revenues from
growth for new resources and recycling techniques to
eliminate our resource constraints? Or should we minimize consumption of material goods by recycling, increasing durability, and changing life styles? In the area
of technology and production the options posed are:
Should we expand production and use the increased revenues to find and apply pollution abatement techniques?
Or should we reduce production and satisfy only the
most basic needs because production is inherently pollut-
ing? Finally, in terms of our social environment and of
the many inequities in the present distribution of wealth
and "quality of life," the options posed are: Should we
continue our growth to provide all men with the ingredients to produce their own versions of the "good" life? Or
should we control growth to narrow the gaps between
the rich and the poor?

These and similar questions by now are familiar. Unfortunately, they cannot be answered meaningfully at the
instrumental level on which they are asked. As Kenneth
Boulding has suggested, our "behavior depends on the
image" (Boulding, 1956, p. 6). In other words, our instrumental decisions reflect our individual and collective images of reality and values. This means that specific policy
issues reflect basic issues which involve conflicts between
different reality and value images. These deeper conflicts
must be resolved before the instrumental issues posed by
the challenge to growth can be addressed. As presented
in this study, a major function of policy research is to develop the procedures and frameworks for identifying the

conflicts between our reality and value images and thus facilitate resolutions of specific policy issues.

Sir Geoffrey Vickers defines Boulding's "image" as the "appreciative setting" developed through the "art of judgment" (Vickers, 1965, p. 67). He identifies the three kinds of judgments involved as reality judgments, value judgments, and instrumental judgments (p. 40). Within this judgmental framework, controversies over growth involve a series of issues at different levels resulting from differences of judgment with respect to physical reality, to values, and to techno-social instruments. The dimensions of these differences, though often more philosophical than policy-oriented, cannot be ignored if policy research is to effect meaningful policy change. Instrumental judgments in policy making must be made within the wider context of these dimensions.

Reality judgments can be placed for our purposes in a spectrum with equilibrium on one side and exponential expansion on the other. Boulding would label the equilibrium image of reality as one of "spaceship earth"; it has limited resources and a fragile ecosystem coinhabited by many forms of life, including a semirational species that technologically tampers with the spaceship to the peril of all aboard. That species itself, however, would judge reality to have the form of exponential expansion; and hold an image of "technological man" having dominion over the earth and all creatures, and free to exploit nature and its resources for whatever goals he might choose.

These two reality judgments differ on the relationship between man and nature, on the quantities and distribution of available resources, on the tolerance of the ecosphere to tampering, and on man's ability to navigate spaceship earth with techno-social instruments. On the operational level of policy planning, where these differences first surface, the challenge to growth has become an emotional issue. Consequently, the arguments too often stress and even exaggerate the differences, but overlook the similarities.

Examination of these reality judgments shows that challenges to growth do not necessarily imply a challenge to all forms of growth. Economic growth in service, cultural, and educational sectors can be encouraged. Technological developments in birth control, pollution abatement, recycling of resources, and alternative energy sources usually are anticipated. In addition, few discourage further economic growth and technological development in developing nations. Similarly, opposing reality judgments do not propose unlimited and unconstrained growth. They do not encourage all forms of economic growth or the development of all technological possibilities.

Thus, the divergent reality judgments contain areas in which agreement on instrumental judgments can be reached or negotiated. If we are to deal with the world macroproblem promptly—which may be tantamount to dealing with it at all—we must seek out these areas of agreement. Simultaneously, the policy researcher must have as one aim the education of the policy maker and of the public in order to create a "shared image" of reality commensurate with the scope of the macroproblem they mutually face.

Value judgments in addition to reality judgments also need to be addressed:

> Consideration of the population issue raises profound questions of what people want, what they need—indeed, what they are for. What does this nation stand for and where is it going? (Commission on

Population Growth and the American Future, 1972, p. 2).

Policy research must illuminate the debate not only over reality judgments—the judgments of "facts"—but also the debate over value judgments of the implications of those facts. This proves to be extremely difficult:

> The value judgments of men and societies cannot be *proved* correct or incorrect; they can only be *approved* as right or *condemned* as wrong by the exercise of another value judgment . . . there are no "external," "objective" criteria (in the narrow sense which we have come to attach to the term) to which appeal can directly be made. In the endless political debate on such matters, which include most of the most vital valuations of our time, each disputant can only expose to the others those aspects of the proposal which he thinks most likely to bring the others' appreciative settings into line with his own (Vickers, 1965, p. 71).

The difficulty can be illustrated by a classification of one important type of value judgment, images of the purpose of life. Some are mutually exclusive; others can be arranged by individuals or societies into hierarchies of values. One classification might be:

> Survival—the ecologist's image
> Enjoyment—the hedonist's image
> Salvation—the missionary's image
> Tradition—the unquestioning image
> Being—the existentialist's image

Each of these images contains a series of dimensions by which the holder defines the "quality of life." Differences in value judgments, then, can be located along dimensions with extremes such as:

> Individual vs. Societal
> Freedom vs. Coercion
> Present vs. Future
> Material vs. Spiritual

Differences in value judgments are located along individual dimensions as well as in the hierarchical ordering of dimensions. Additional complications to be considered are that value judgments within dimensions and among hierarchies change over time and often are internally inconsistent.

Policy makers in the years ahead will face the need to develop consensus about specific instrumental policies from individuals and groups with increasingly divergent value judgments of the purpose and quality of life. Reasoned instrumental judgments will not be possible on the basis of traditional American values because exponential growth has provoked challenges to the growth ethic from numerous points of view. Realizing the extent of the macroproblem, many persons have refocused their images of reality. Consequently, they question the traditional value images of equity, individual freedom, responsibility, quantity, consumption, and even of beauty. The new value images are incompatible with growth-oriented instrumental policies.

Instrumental judgments are where policy decisions are made. Yet, instrumental judgments require the ability to make reality and value judgments. Policy makers—public or private, individuals or groups—assume or actually make reality judgments as to what is, value judgments as to what should be, and instrumental judgments as to how to bring reality judgments and value judgments into reasonably close agreement. Unfortunately, because instrumental judgments require the setting of priorities, planning, funding, opportunity costs, innovation and change, issues most often are debated only at the level of instrumental judgments. Instrumental judgments are, of course, critically important and should be debated. But at the instrumental level, reality and value judgments, the core assumptions underlying policy decisions, often go unchallenged. Disjointed incrementalism, the policy-making process so antithetical to the process we suggest in this study, in fact operates just at the instrumental level. Policy researchers should delineate and challenge core assumptions (Etzioni, 1971); it is here they can complement the decision makers.

The diverse range of reality and value judgments now emerging make instrumental judgments with respect to growth, population, consumption, and technology a matter requiring a comprehensive decision-making process. Until we weigh the tolerance of the environment to various forms of disruption, we can expect little agreement on controls. Until we investigate the relationship between population growth and our ability to achieve individual and collective goals, we can expect little agreement on population size and distribution. Until we accept the limitations of technology and redefine its capabilities for preserving and creating resources while avoiding environmental degradation, we can expect little agreement on desirable levels of aggregate and per capita consumption. Until we have the institutions, the desire, and the ability to manage ourselves and our technologies equitably and humanely, we cannot begin to solve the macroproblem. Until we to some extent share reality images and until we agree on certain value judgments, we cannot expect to agree on instrumental judgments to relieve the pressures on the world ecosystem.

Chapter III

The Ecosystem Image and Its Policy Implications

The ability to formulate effective policy depends on the accuracy and scope of the policy maker's image of reality. The world macroproblem as we perceive it indicates the inadequacy of the image of reality upon which much of our past policy has been built. Many past policy decisions considered the social, political, and economic impacts without paying adequate attention to the environmental and resource impacts. Consequently, the linkages between the impacts of the actions taken and these other factors of the ecosystem have been considered only casually, if at all. For example, the degradation of Lake Erie, smog in Los Angeles, or DDT in milk results in part from the policy maker's failure to consider fundamental linkages within the ecosystem.

Such environmental feedback dramatizes the need to enlarge our image of reality. Our society in fact already has started to meet this need. The requirement in the National Environmental Policy Act of 1969 of environmental impact statements for every relevant proposed federal legislation and action is an attempt on the part of policy makers to enlarge our image. Similarly, the approach on the part of economists to internalize externalities is an attempt to make the price system, which has a critically important effect on the working of our society, also reflect this wider image. The development of ecology courses at the elementary school level will significantly enlarge our collective image of reality in the long run.

Effective decision making on the macrosystem level requires the inclusion of the fundamental ecosystem linkages in policy research and deliberations. To that end we propose a comprehensive ecosystem image to provide the framework necessary for policy research and policy decisions commensurate with the scope of the world macroproblem. Such an image embodies the reality, value, and instrumental judgments we have used to define this macroproblem.

We construct our ecosystem image on the basis of the four major subsystems of the ecosphere: the atmosphere, the lithosphere, the hydrosphere, and the biosphere. In addition, within the biosphere we delineate one further subsystem, the "hominisphere." We define the "hominisphere" as that subsystem of the biosphere which includes social and cultural institutions as well as the production and technology components peculiar to man as a species.

Two distinctive features of the hominisphere are of particular importance to the dynamics of the entire ecosystem. First, man is increasing his influence on the other components of the ecosystem. Second, man is the only organism to plan and implement policies consciously, with respect to itself and the rest of the ecosystem. These features make the hominisphere, within certain ecosystemic constraints, a dynamic, self-directing, cybernetic system.

Our basic premise is that policy research must take place with a comprehensive image of the ecosystem and of man's activity with respect to the rest of the ecosystem. Policy decision must develop the welfare of the hominisphere without damage to the linkages within the ecosystem. Policy makers must develop an awareness of the interactions of the hominisphere variables with variables throughout the entire ecosystem. Such an awareness requires the construction of a comprehensive ecosystem image.

The determination of the important hominisphere variables which interact with variables in the four major subsystems of the ecosphere reflects reality and value judgments on the part of those making the determination. On the basis of the ecosystem image we have constructed and of the macroproblem as we perceive it, we identify four key variables within the hominisphere: (1) population size; (2) population distribution; (3) per capita resource consumption; and (4) technology. In identifying these variables, we are in general agreement with The Commission on Population Growth and the American Future (1972, pp. 56–57):

> The pressure that this nation puts on resources and the environment during the next 30 to 50 years will depend on the size of the national population, the size of population in local areas, the amounts and types of goods and services the population consumes, and the ways in which these goods and services are produced, used, and disposed of. All these factors are important. Right now, because of our large population size and high economic productivity, the United States puts more pressure on resources and the environment than any other nation in the world.

As the President's Commission suggests, no single variable manipulated in isolation will yield a solution to the world macroproblem of concern here. The problems result from the interaction of all four of these key variables within our society's institutional frameworks. Amitai Etzioni would call them "malleable" variables (Etzioni,

1971, p. 11), and we have referred to them as leverage variables in figure 2. These malleable variables are those which can be adjusted by policy decisions to alter the impacts of the hominisphere on the rest of the ecosystem. To be meaningful and effective, these decisions must embody a comprehensive image of reality. The decision makers must consider the interactions and tradeoffs between all of these leverage variables and their impacts upon the ecosystem.

Such comprehensive thinking requires the systematic construction of an ecosystem image before policy research can proceed effectively. There are simply too many variables, too many linkages, too many uncertainties, too many alternatives, and too many points of view for the policy maker to operate solely with intuitively constructed images. In addition, as the complexity of the image increases, the abilities of our individual and collective minds to comprehend the problems rationally and to devise solutions are pressed to the limit. Therefore, policy makers must learn to place more emphasis on the kinds of analytical modeling and simulation discussed in chapter 5 of this study. A systems approach with its analytic and methodological tools can help the policy maker to find and assess the inconsistencies and conflicts among his reality, value, and instrumental judgments. Such an approach for instrumental action, however, cannot be taken until a comprehensive ecosystem reality image is constructed. This we do next by classifying the relevant impacts and policies within the framework of the entire ecosystem of the Earth—the ecosphere.

Classification of Impacts

The classification of impacts and policies is beneficial to decision makers in at least four ways. First, classification schemes conveniently locate pertinent policies (that is, provide a filing technique) for relatively easy identification, finding, and reference. Second, classification of impacts and policies indicates relationships and provides a basis for comparison of different impacts and different policies. Without a classification system, decision makers could overlook alternative policies or could fail to account for the system interactions that would influence implementation of a policy. Third, classification provides a framework for communication and the building of alliances across existing institutional barriers. Fourth, and perhaps most important, a classification scheme allows the planner to conceptualize and manipulate models of the relationships among various parts of the ecosystem.

The environmental crisis of concern to us and to future decision makers has arisen from the interaction between man (the human sociocultural and production system—the hominisphere) and the four great and interlinked natural systems that compose ecosystem Earth (the ecosphere): (1) air (the atmosphere); (2) water (the hydrosphere); (3) earth crust (the lithosphere); and (4) living organisms (the biosphere, which includes the hominisphere). It should be noted that we use the term "ecosphere," a term coined by La Mont Cole, for what traditional ecologists call the "biosphere" (Odum, 1971, pp. 11–16). For purposes of emphasis, we have chosen to include only living creatures in the biosphere.

The hominisphere is but a single and, in geological time, the very newest part of the complex web of ecosystemic interdependencies that function as the ecosphere. Yet this human sphere has become increasingly dominant and pervasive in its impacts upon the four interlinked natural systems—upon the natural functions on which man is so vitally dependent. His rise to ecological dominance means man has continually expanded his functional niche in the ecosphere; that is, he has expanded both his control and changes of function in the ecosphere. This continued expansion of human influence has produced quantitative and qualitative changes in and among the other parts of the ecosphere. Classification of these impacts provides a method of defining the impact space for policy research purposes.

Development of a comprehensive ecosystem image involves delineation of these systems of linkages which describe the transformation in the mapping of alternative policies from the policy space to the impact space. Classification of policies and impacts within such an ecosystem framework is extremely adaptable because (1) the earth ecosystem image is all-inclusive, and (2) all policies, population and otherwise, are subject to the constraints of the ecosphere (fig. 5). An ecosystem includes all factors within specified boundaries—biological factors, physical factors, sociocultural factors, etc. An ecosystem can be as small as a raindrop or as large as the universe, depending upon the boundaries set by the concept user. For this classification scheme, the ecosystem is considered to be the proximity of the Earth.

This ecosystem, as we define it, must be distinguished from the more limited concept some persons have of ecosystem Earth. Their image of the ecosystem includes only "natural" phenomena (e.g., birds, trees, the hydrocycle, etc.). They do not include the sociocultural activities and institutions of man. The ecosystem image as we use it in this study must include *all* manifestations of life on Earth if it is to be useful to policy planners.

In fact, our ecosystem scheme implicitly assumes that man can control the ecosystem for his own maximum benefit only through maintenance of the integrity of the

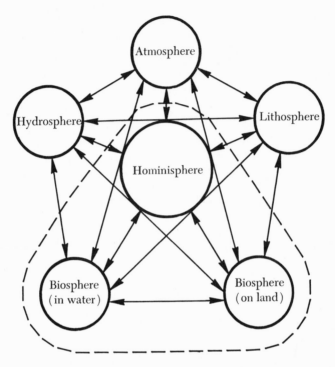

Fig. 5. Ecosystem earth (the ecosphere), showing interactive linkages of the component subsystems (adapted from White, Lagler *et al.*, 1972). The dashes enclose the biosphere.

ecosystem. This idea is succinctly expressed by land-use architect Ian McHarg (1970, p. 23): "The role of man is to understand nature . . . and to intervene to enhance its creative processes. He is the prospective steward of the biosphere."

As figure 5 demonstrates, man subjectively perceives himself as the center of the ecosphere. To be steward of the estate he must include himself in his image of reality.

By adopting an ecosystemic framework for the classification of impacts, we eliminate more restrictive schemes of population-environment impact classification based upon narrower categories such as cultural institutions or geographical location (Russell and Landsberg, 1971). These more limited categories appear *within* our scheme as parts of the ecosystem. Locating more specialized categories within a larger framework will lead decision makers to consider the ramifications of proposed policies in an enlarged context. Specifying interactions with the larger framework could prompt decision makers to improve assessment of various impact areas by seeking expert counsel and could minimize the likelihood of gross oversights. Furthermore, since significant ecosystem changes usually are long-term in nature, the comprehensive ecosystem view could stimulate decision makers to consider the long-term population and environment interactions that consistently have been ignored up to the present time. This ecosystem approach also will broaden the public's perception of man-environment.

The skeleton chart (fig. 6) itemizes the interacting components of the major subsystems of the ecosphere: the atmosphere, the lithosphere, the hydrosphere, and the biosphere. It also helps to show the significance of the hominisphere in the biosphere with a selected display of institutions and activities peculiar to humans.

We position the human activity subsystem vertically between the environmental support subsystems. The components of the hominisphere interact horizontally with all the itemized components and conditions of the other four subsystems. Components also interact vertically within a subsystem, especially in the form of feedback loops. We focus on horizontal interactions, however, in order to acquaint decision makers with subsystem relationships they previously may not have considered. (The

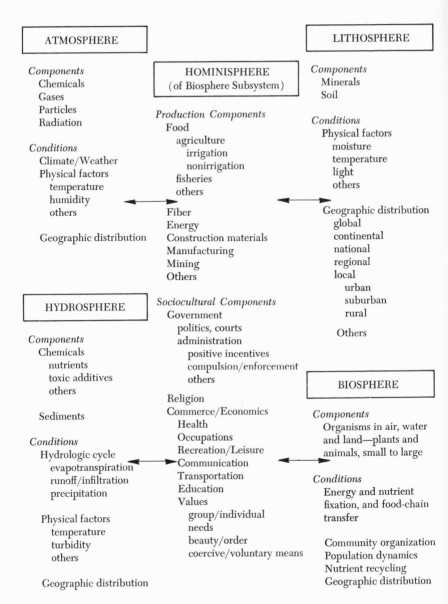

Fig. 6. An ecosystem for the classification of impacts, where components of the hominisphere affect the components and conditions of the other spheres.

vertical format of the components does not imply a hierarchy of importance; it is only for convenience). Although we could delineate the components and subcomponents of each system further, the breakdown we present adequately serves to illustrate the application of the classification scheme.

Since subsystem components are all interrelated, the many pervasive connecting linkages have not been drawn. All of the interrelationships are not of equal importance, however, whether assessed from the viewpoint of maintaining ecosystem integrity or of maximizing linkages particularly important to humans. For example, an interaction set representative of primary linkages is shown in figure 7:

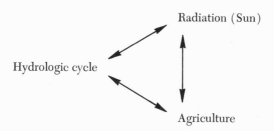

Fig. 7. Diagrammatic representation of primary ecosystem linkages.

Other relationship sets can be termed secondary or tertiary, depending upon system characteristics and classification values.

This concept of different levels of linkages of varying importance is analogous to the concept of "economic linkages," where industries more basic to the economy (e.g., steel) are considered as "primary" industries and those using steel as raw material for manufacturing are considered as "secondary" industries. Such levels of linkages enable us to classify impacts most appropriately. Impacts that adversely affect primary linkages are the ones most perilous for man (as well as for the ecosystem); these impacts are to be avoided. Conversely, impacts that affect tertiary or quaternary linkages point to variables that policy makers can manipulate more freely with less risk.

Primary linkages and impacts, at least over short time periods, usually can be identified without undue effort. The relative contributions of the primary interaction components, however, cannot be so easily identified. Statistical correlation coefficients do not show causality, although their use may indicate those factors that are important to maintaining system linkages. Assuming that relevant system data could be obtained, perhaps statistical methods such as regression analysis techniques could disclose those subsystem components responsible for the greatest amount of variance of the primary linkages. Those responsible for the greatest variance would be the most crucial to maintenance of the natural condition of the interaction linkages. Thus, those components should be given priority in the decision-making tradeoffs, as discussed in chapter 5 under "Criteria for Selection Among Policy Alternatives."

Such considerations are premature here. The major function of this ecosystem classification scheme is to show interrelationships, not to offer a logic for making choices. The problem of impact assessment is addressed after the interrelationships are determined.

In the ecosystem classification scheme, impacts are classified according to the subcomponent category where the greatest impact can be expected. Determination of the best classification category requires consideration of the interactions among all the subsystems.

One example of impact classification is that of automobiles, which traditionally has involved categories within the hominisphere. When the impact of automobiles is placed within the more comprehensive ecosystem classification scheme, more extensive interactions are delineated. Consideration of auto impacts from an ecosystemic perspective involves many other components, including those shown in figure 8.

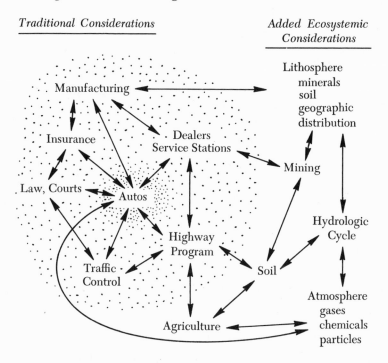

Fig. 8. Traditional concept of automobile impacts (stippled area) and display of added ecosystemic considerations.

Even though the impact is classified in the transportation category of the hominisphere (fig. 6), ecosystemic classification elucidates a variety of additional relationships and impacts. This ecosystemic approach, furthermore, points toward possible areas of future impacts. The policy maker's image of reality must be based on this ecosystem scheme if he is to develop problem solutions that maintain "the integrity of the ecosystem" in the face of environmental impacts of automobiles.

Classification of Policies

Once the ecosystem classification scheme has been used to define the dimensions of the impact space, we need to classify policies within the policy space in terms of the leverage variables which affect the linkages within the ecosphere. The leverage variables are "malleable" variables of the hominisphere which react significantly with the variables in the four subsystems of the ecosphere. The leverage variables, identified previously, are (1) population size; (2) population distribution; (3) resource consumption; and (4) technology. These variables provide the categories for a conceptual framework for identification and analysis of relevant policies by decision makers.

A policy consists of a set of guidelines used to pursue a specified goal. In a society, such goals are always either directly or indirectly concerned with quality of living. Although the word "quality" has an imprecise connotation, its meaning is far from being nebulous, since any given quality reflects a sum of components interacting in a particular sequence over a time span. For example, the suburban lifestyle has a set of components (e.g., population density, open space, and residential housing patterns) that give it a distinctive quality. We propose to expand the definition of "quality" to the scope of the ecosphere so that the concept of "quality" will include such attributes as integrity of primary linkages in the major subsystems, as discussed earlier. Such factors as population growth, population distribution, resource consumption, technology and production, and institutional arrangements all affect our quality of life.

Some persons relate degenerating environmental quality to the increasing number of people, considering degeneration a product of population growth (Ehrlich, 1971). Others suggest the congestion of cities, implying that the problem relates to the spatial distribution of people (Harte and Socolow, 1971). Some persons today attack practices, such as waste accumulation, associated with resource consumption (Coale, 1970), or blame technology for contributing to the exponential degradation of the ecosphere (Commoner, 1971). Recently, a few persons have started to discuss the inadequacies in governmental and other institutional planning practices that contribute to the degenerating process (Fitch, 1968).

Our classification scheme enables us to apportion the responsibility for the degeneration of the environment in varying degrees among all the factors. The systems approach will show that this analysis must be followed by consideration of the policy-making process in order to account for the institutional arrangements which pervade the overall procedure.

The classification scheme first places each of the population-environment policies in the most appropriate of the four categories previously designated. The policies are then analyzed in terms of descriptive elements derived from the three types of judgments discussed previously—reality, value, and instrumental. For application purposes we label the judgmental categories of descriptive elements as: ecosystem interactions, value premises, and operational considerations (fig. 9).

The "ecosystem interaction" elements estimate the extent of environmental impacts a policy is expected to exert. The "value premise" elements indicate the degree

Policy Categories / Judgmental Categories of Descriptive Elements	Population Size	Population Distribution	Resource Consumption	Technology
Ecosystem Interactions				
Value Premises				
Operational Considerations				

Fig. 9. Classification matrix for policy analysis.

to which a policy reflects selected values of the society. (Different societies and subcultures in each society have different prevailing values, of course.) The "operational consideration" elements specify items of practical concern to decision makers, such as estimated costs of a policy and the predicted acceptance of a policy by the public. Some specific elements within each of these three categories are discussed below.

The classification scheme further provides each descriptive element within the three judgmental categories with a grading scale based upon a range of alternatives, bounded by opposing concepts (e.g., short—long). As used for illustrative purposes (fig. 10) these elements and their scales are not all-inclusive; they are only representative of the kinds of elements that can be used to classify policies under this scheme.

DESCRIPTIVE ELEMENTS	POLICY CATEGORY
	(e.g., Population Size)

Ecosystem Interactions

1. Estimate of the degree of ecosystem interactions or impacts — low ⟶ high

Value Premises

2. Means to obtain policy objectives — coercive ⟶ voluntary
3. Freedoms fostered by the policy — collective ⟶ self-actualization
4. Policy relative to needs hierarchy — basic (food, security) ⟶ individual fulfillment
5. Conduciveness to beauty and/or order — low ⟶ high
6. Implementation modes of the policy — competition ⟶ cooperation

Operational Considerations

7. Time-span focus — short ⟶ long
8. Geographic location — community ⟶ global
9. Cost (relative to alternatives) — high ⟶ low
10. Public participation in decision-making processes — low ⟶ high
11. Stage of policy — data collection ⟶ implementation
12. Degree of flexibility and diversity permitted by the policy — low ⟶ high
13. Availability of implementation vehicles — unavailable ⟶ ready
14. Predicted acceptance by the public — low ⟶ high
15. Predicted acceptance by government — low ⟶ high
16. Projected potential for mass communication — low ⟶ high

Fig. 10. Matrix for classifying policies. (A hypothetical policy concerning abortion clinics is used to illustrate the grading [0] of selected descriptive elements of the policy.)

The category of descriptive elements related to the total ecosystem image, "ecosystem interactions" (fig. 10, item 1), indicates the general extent of expected policy interactions and impacts. This criterion should stimulate decision makers to consider the full ramifications of a policy, and especially to do so when high degrees of ecosystemic interactions and impacts are indicated. This judgmental category ideally would be expanded to include descriptive elements comprehending the impacts of a policy on the primary and other linkages in the four subsystems of the ecosphere, as discussed above.

The category of descriptive elements related to the image of "value premises" classifies the policies according to selected values deemed central to the Western cultural heritage, such as security-survival, freedom, and justice (Callahan, 1972). The relevance of the selected values to the future needs and goals of the country has not been determined here, and constitutes an area for future research.

A number of methods can be used to derive the values selected for inclusion in the classification scheme, including the Delphi technique and opinion surveys. A Delphi exercise can ascertain the opinion of experts on the choices of values. A survey of representative constituencies in the policy's impact space can also be used to indicate the value implications of the policy.

Following the selection of relevant values, specific descriptive elements embedded in the values need to be identified. Disaggregation methods (Stanford Research Institute, 1969) could be used to reveal the opposing concepts that form the basis for grading scales. The disaggregation of freedom and security-survival values is shown in figure 11, which also indicates how these disaggregated values can be used to construct the grading scales used in the classification matrix.

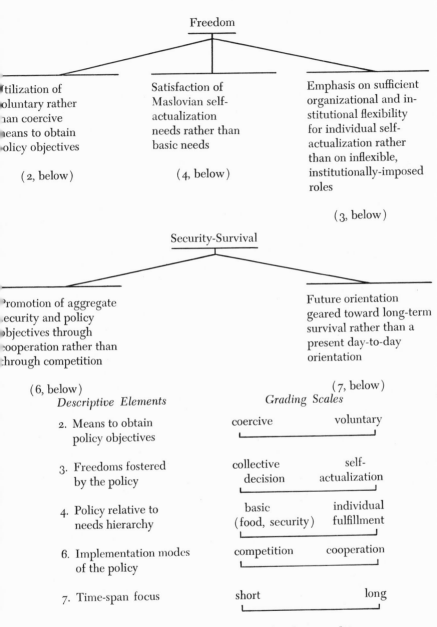

Freedom

Utilization of
voluntary rather
than coercive
means to obtain
policy objectives

(2, below)

Satisfaction of
Maslovian self-
actualization
needs rather than
basic needs

(4, below)

Emphasis on sufficient
organizational and in-
stitutional flexibility
for individual self-
actualization rather
than on inflexible,
institutionally-imposed
roles

(3, below)

Security-Survival

Promotion of aggregate
security and policy
objectives through
cooperation rather than
through competition

(6, below)

Future orientation
geared toward long-term
survival rather than a
present day-to-day
orientation

(7, below)

Descriptive Elements   *Grading Scales*

2. Means to obtain   coercive   voluntary
   policy objectives

3. Freedoms fostered   collective   self-
   by the policy   decision   actualization

4. Policy relative to   basic   individual
   needs hierarchy   (food, security)   fulfillment

6. Implementation modes   competition   cooperation
   of the policy

7. Time-span focus   short   long

Fig. 11. Disaggregation of abstract social values, and incorpo-
ration into grading scales (on fig. 10).

The classification of elements based on *value prem-ises* includes the following, items 2 to 6 in figure 10:

2. Means to obtain policy objectives; this scale ranges from coercive to voluntary means.

3. Freedoms fostered by the policy—this value scale with collective decisions and self-actualization as its boundaries neither implies that individual expression can be achieved in the total absence of social (collective) constraints nor vice versa. The opportunity and manner of development of the individual is always subject to the basic collective goals of the society, and of course is conditioned by the social images the individual receives. This descriptive element emphasizes the extent to which the fate of the individual is affected by collective decision.

4. Policy relative to needs hierarchy, that is, toward the perceived needs of the society. Various social psychologists (e.g., Maslow, 1970) argue that human needs are hierarchically arranged from basic physiological and security needs to higher level ego and self-fulfillment needs, with the basic needs usually taking immediate precedence over higher ones. A policy classification in terms of hierarchical needs indicates the stage of social development of the individual(s) affected by the policy.

5. Conduciveness to beauty and/or order, as these terms are defined philosophically.

6. Implementation modes of the policy, that is, whether the policy assumes cooperation or competition as a means for implementation.

The category of descriptive elements related to *instrumental judgment,* "operational considerations," (items

7 to 16 in fig. 10) contains policy elements most familiar to decision makers:

7. Time span focus—the period of time over which the policy is designed to function.

8. Geographic location in which the policy is to be used.

9. Cost (relative to alternatives)—the estimated cost of implementation of the policy at the time the policy is classified.

10. Public participation in decision-making processes; this participation is a factor of governmental and social institutional structures.

11. Stage of policy—the stage of the problem-solving process where the policy is directed (e.g., data collection, implementation methods).

12. Degree of flexibility and diversity permitted by the policy—in general, diversity and flexibility are to be desired because they favor system adaptability and therefore stability.

13. Availability of implementation vehicles—resources, new technologies, institutional arrangements, etc., necessary for implementation of the policy.

14. Predicted acceptance by the public of the policy, a matter of degree measured by social indicators.

15. Predicted acceptance by government—the extent to which various government officials will embrace the plans.

16. Projected potential for mass communication of the policy decisions—dissemination to the public at large.

Since many of the items of this scheme require relative judgments (e.g., the degree of flexibility permitted by the policy), it will be necessary to minimize bias and maintain uniform standards. If the classification scheme is administered by a central agency, these difficulties can, with effort, be alleviated.

Such a classification scheme for analysis of policies will need to be updated continually. It will have to be adjusted to changing social conditions, to changing images and values, and to changing conditions in and understandings of the ecosphere. Of particular concern will be the changing policy-making environment, as discussed in chapter 6. The policy-making process, therefore, must provide for periodic review at specified intervals of the classification scheme used for policy analysis and evaluation in the planning stage.

One unique feature of this scheme (fig. 10) allows an initial comprehensive evaluation of policy alternatives. Because of the way in which the analysis scales are structured, the locations of the choices on the scales generally reflect the pattern of social development of the culture. For example, the grades on the extreme right of the chart reflect "world-wide orientation," a "high degree of voluntary cooperation," a "long time-span focus" and "macroeconomic efficiency"—a pattern associated with the development of the ecosystem image discussed above. The polar alternatives on the extreme left indicate "parochial outlooks," "earlier policy implementation stages," and "preoccupation with physiological human needs." Thus, an initial judgment of the contribution of a policy to the construction of a viable ecosystem image can be determined quickly from the distribution of points on the value scales of the classification matrix. Many issues are situational, however. For instance, a competitive situation may be preferred over the short run, while cooperation may be desired for long-range goals. Consequently, this unique left-right matrix organization only has general applicability.

An advantage of this classification scheme over other attempts at classifying such policies as population policy is evident when this advance scheme is compared with a typical scheme, as illustrated in figure 12, which evaluates a family-planning policy. Based upon a format developed by Berelson (1969), the typical scheme does not elucidate as much information as does the proposed matrix scheme, nor does it as quickly indicate overall trends. In addition, our matrix scheme presumably would be developed in much greater detail for actual use.

The classically typical assessment scheme, illustrated in figure 12, can be contrasted to the example of our classification matrix applied to a hypothetical federal policy on abortion clinics. In the matrix classification scheme (fig. 10), the symbol 0, located on the grading scales, is used in evaluation of the descriptive elements. Although all of the elements have not been utilized in the following abortion clinic example, enough are shown to illustrate the operation of the matrix scheme.

For example, assume that the federal government adopts a policy which establishes federally funded abortion clinics to be made operational over the next five years at the invitation of communities following local referenda. Application of the value-premises categories indicates that the policy involves voluntary public participation from the initial stages.

Operational considerations indicate that the policy has a moderately short time span but has a national focus. Since medical services are undergoing rapid cost increases, the cost of the program also is likely to be high. A moderate degree of policy flexibility is inherent in permitting local options. In addition, since other governmental bodies such as state governments have had experience in operating abortion programs, implementation vehicles

DESCRIPTIVE ELEMENT	ASSESSMENT
Impact on Subgroups	Greater equality of opportunity to prevent unwanted births.
Effect on Direction	Downward.
Magnitude	Approximately 10% reduction.

Recent Government Action	*Legislative:*
	Provide monies to state and local public and private agencies to provide services.
	
	Administrative:
	1. Health department leadership to help provide the most effective means of providing services and in eliminating barriers listed above.
	
	2. Repeal of restrictions on:
	   a) advertisement and distribution of nonprescription contraceptives;
	
	   b) teaching of birth control methods in public schools.
	
	3. Requirement that all hospitals with maternity service perform appropriate sterilizing operations without discrimination as to age, parity, or sex.

Other Effects	1. Encourages entry into the preventive health-care system. 2. Allows acceptors to experience effects of planning ahead. 3. Improves maternal, child, and family health.

Acceptability:
  Public
  Legislators
	
	High
	High

Fig. 12. Example of an earlier, typical approach at categorizing and grading a policy on the extension of family planning through full provision of family-planning services (adapted from Oakley and Corsa, 1971).

should be available. Furthermore, since the birth rate has been declining, even in the absence of official government sanction, general public acceptance could be moderately high. Since abortion has a history of controversy, the policy has a high projected potential for mass communication (perhaps, however, with information distortion).

An initial analysis of the classification pattern applied to the abortion-policy example reveals that a preponderance of classification gravitates to the right side of the matrix scheme (fig. 10). This indicates that such a policy is a viable alternative within the comprehensive framework of an ecosystem image. By way of contrast, the implication for ecological interactions of the family-planning policy illustrated in figure 12 is not immediately apparent. Consequently, a matrix such as ours for classifying policies based on a comprehensive ecosystem view can lead effectively to deepened investigations of the potential ramifications of a proposed policy.

Chapter IV

Policy Menu and Deliberation

The ecosystem image is used to define the dimensions of the impact space of policies (figs. 1 and 2), which are then classified within the policy space in terms of leverage variables. The policies used to manipulate these leverage variables now need to be considered in more detail, for practical deliberations and decisions can be made only at the level of specific policies. As we get into practical details, each of the leverage variables will be broken down into lower-level variables which will suggest or be more directly coupled to specific policy decisions. For example, the leverage variable of population size can be broken down to include the rates of birth, death, immigration, and emigration. The leverage variable of resource consumption can be broken down to include lower-level per capita consumption of minerals, fuels, etc., and per capita generation of waste products. The nature of these variables, their relationships to the corresponding leverage variables as well as to one another, and their coupling to specific policies must be delineated in order to generate a reasonably wide range of specific offerings in the menu for policy deliberations.

Another useful way to create new policies for the policy menu is to analyze present policies from a deliberately critical stance (Etzioni, 1971). We have suggested an ecosystem perspective for policy analysis. In this perspective, the hominisphere sustains itself by consuming the ecosphere's resources, and, through technology and production, by transforming many of them into goods, wastes, and services. The impact of this process has been greatly enlarged by the exponential growth of population. As the hominisphere grows, it becomes increasingly dominant within the ecosphere. The size and rate of this growth threatens ecosystem integrity; of equal importance is the manner by which this growth is sustained and even accelerated. Growth in production is promoted by large-scale technological developments, institutional and organizational changes toward centralized control, and concentration of population distribution.

The important changes in the ecosystem being produced by these developments within the hominisphere are not yet fully understood. They create environmental problems which demand new *modes* of policy responses. No longer can we tacitly assume that, with restructured economic incentives, the macroproblem will find its own solution. No longer can we blithely look to technology as a panacea to the scarcity or limits of resources.

To generate new policies consistent with the ecosystem image, we will begin with ecosystem integrity as a major constraint. The long-term as well as short-term consequences of violating this constraint would be consciously included in the calculus of the total cost of any specific policy. A systems approach is the best known way to guide long-term developments of technology and socioeconomic institutions and to guide long-term population growth and distribution. This approach contrasts with the piecemeal, disjointed incremental approach by which prevailing policies have been generated. If growth of population and resource consumption threaten ecosystem integrity, and policy makers cannot devise reliable and satisfactory technological solutions, then policies curtailing growth will need to be seriously and promptly considered. Such new policies must be implemented with sufficient lead time to achieve maximum compatibility with basic social values.

In the following, we will consider four policy categories: population size, population distribution, resource consumption, and technology. For each of these categories, we will discuss the nature of the policy variables, the core assumptions of prevailing policies, new modes of policy response, and some alternative policies. Although the alternative policies are not necessarily better or worse than prevailing policies, as the judgment of specific policies is multifarious, many of them would be more consistent than present policies with the ecosystem perspective of the reality image we are constructing.

Policy on Population Size
The total population size is generally recognized as a leverage variable in the context of the world macroproblem. However, this leverage variable needs to be subdivided into lower-level variables, such as fertility rate, migration rate, and composition in terms of age, sex, race, etc., for detailed study of the specific impacts of population on the ecosystem and of the specific policies that can affect population size. One researcher, for example, has defined and characterized an optimum population, specifying a low level of mortality, a stable age and sex distribution, and a secular growth rate equal to zero (Day, 1969).

Although some people speak of living space as the ultimate spatial constraint to unlimited population growth, nobody expects this constraint to become active. The ecosphere will become uninhabitable long before the spatial constraint sets in. Population size per se has much less impact on the ecosystem than the synergic impact exerted by population size and per capita resource consumption. For this reason, total population should be broken down into its subcomponents in terms of age, race, and socioeconomic classes, each with its resource consumption implications, if the synergic impact on the ecosystem is to be studied in detail. Similarly, analysis of the shifting life styles, values, and beliefs, especially in terms of their compatibility with the ecosystem image inherent in the population subcomponents, will be useful for impact studies.

Analysis of the subcomponents of population size is also useful for considering specific policies and policy menu offerings. In forecasting population changes, the gross birth rate (number of births per 1,000 people) and death rate are much less meaningful than the age composition and the age-specific fertility rate (number of births per 1,000 women in a specific age bracket) and age-specific death rate. With the latter information, one can understand why the United States population will continue to grow for a long time, even if the fertility rate reaches the replacement rate of 2.1 children per family, and why immediate and continued zero population growth would require an instant drop below the replacement rate and a fluctuation around that rate over time. In the same vein, the breakdown of population size into ethnic and racial components will help policy researchers forecast population changes from race-specific data and will help them understand certain political issues in population policy planning. Relative population sizes usually are perceived to represent the relative political power of various groups in a multi-ethnic society.

The relationship between population size and the

lower-level variables (fertility rate, death rate, migration rate, etc.) is straightforward mathematics, although the mathematics is by no means simple (Keyfitz, 1968). The relationship between the lower-level variables, however, especially fertility rate and specific policy decisions, is poorly understood in spite of a large amount of previous research on the subject. Some hold the view that population size adjusts itself naturally to environmental conditions. We do know that fertility is significantly influenced by the socioeconomic environment, but the exact nature of this dependence is unclear. One hypothesis suggests that fertility declines with the progress of socioeconomic development. A plot of fertility rate versus per capita GNP based on United States historical data, however, showed that the function is not even monotonic (Glass and Watt, 1971). Therefore, although the recent trend of the United States fertility rate has been declining toward the replacement rate, there is no assurance that this decline is not a temporary dip.

The United States government position with respect to population size has undergone substantial changes. As recently as 1959 President Eisenhower made it an explicit position for the government to refrain from involvement in any family-planning programs. By contrast, in setting up the Commission on Population Growth and the American Future, President Nixon stated in 1969: "One of the most serious challenges to human destiny in the last third of this century will be the growth of the population. Whether man's response to that challenge will be a cause for pride or for despair in the year 2000 will depend very much on what we do today" (*Report*, p. 3).

Despite that statement, there is yet no explicit United States policy on population size. The implicit policy seems to be that the current trend of population size

judged alone in isolation from population distribution, resource consumption, and technology. Depending on how these other three leverage variables are manipulated, population size can increase, be stabilized, or even reduced. In this context the policy menu must be expanded beyond its current limitation to family planning services.

The expansion of the policy menu would include the consideration of intensified educational campaigns, positive incentive programs to encourage conscious attempts to maintain family size at some optimum level, tax and welfare benefits and penalties, establishment of involuntary fertility control, and other means such as shifts in social and economic institutions (Berelson, 1969). In this expansion even policies such as the use of temporary sterilants (Ehrlich, 1968) would not be dismissed at the outset, although these policies probably would be screened out later after serving the purpose of pointing out possible consequences if more desirable policies are not implemented sooner.

Among the policies in the expanded menu, there is little doubt that at present the most "cost-effective" way of manipulating the population size variable is by means of family planning techniques. Since nearly 20 percent of recent births in the United States were unwanted, the elimination of unwanted births (with "perfect" family planning) could substantially reduce our future growth rate (Bumpass, Westoff, 1970). A number of conditions, however, could require the adoption of more costly measures. If, for example, there occurred a marked increase in the average number of children desired, then family planning techniques oriented to eliminating unwanted would not be effective. Similarly, if perceptions of the severity of the problem changed and it should determined that the size of the total population must implementa be reduced (meaning a fertility rate less than replacement), more comprehensive policies would be needed.

It is certainly true that "because population is the most difficult and slowest to yield among the components of environmental deterioration," we must implement effective population planning policies immediately (Ehrlich and Holdren, 1971, p. 1216). The question of *where* to start is relatively easy to answer. We must start with family planning because this is the most acceptable means of affecting population size. Furthermore, family planning programs (those programs oriented to reducing the number of unwanted births) are an essential instrument through which other proposals (to reduce the number of births desired) take effect. In order to reduce fertility by changing the motivation as to family size, it is also necessary to provide the means by which the unwanted births can be averted. So, where to start is not a difficult policy question. The difficulties are encountered when determining how and how far to go beyond family planning.

After we expand the policy menu as suggested above, the specific policies on population size could be deliberated according to the judgmental categories of descriptive elements as listed in figure 10. Complete deliberations, however, will not be easy for a number of reasons. Fertility control is in the most sensitive realm of human attitude and behavior, and is, consequently, difficult to control, predict, or even study. One can analyze and identify which government policies appear to be pronatal (encourage childbearing). One could suggest new policies to subsidize or encourage small families, to encourage greater employment of women, and to promote vigorously ZPG as the ultimate goal. It remains uncertain, however, as to what actual decline of fertility rate would result from the abolishment of pronatalist policies and the establishment of antinatalist policies. Therefore, to expand the policy space significantly, we need research into the social, cultural, and environmental factors that affect fertility. Examples of such research are "The Value of Children to Parents" by Lois Hoffman in *Psychological Prospects on Population* (1973) and "Low Income Families: Fertility Changes in the 1960's" by Frederick S. Jaffe in *Family Planning Perspectives*. Meanwhile, the policy decisions must be made in the face of a high degree of uncertainty.

In conclusion, policy on population size per se is meaningless unless it is considered in an ecosystem framework along with the other three related types of policies. Within that framework, the menu for population size should be expanded beyond the current policy focus on family planning. In view of the very imperfect knowledge of the effectiveness of various population-planning programs and the lack of acceptance of the ecosystem image by the public, the policy issues surrounding population size will continue to be controversial in the near future. Given this situation, the need is evident for policy-making organizations to support uncertainty acknowledgment, error-embracing, goal setting, and feedback soliciting, as will be discussed in chapter 6.

Policy on Population Distribution
The nature of the population distribution leverage variable has changed with the disproportional growth of the technological system in the hominisphere. Human societies historically have responded to the pressures of population growth on the environment by redistributing their populations. The redistribution in pretechnological societies took the form of large-scale migration of surplus pop-

ulation to uninhabited areas from areas where population growth threatened the stability of the ecosystem. These new areas, in addition, often exerted the magnetic attraction of improved survival and comfort and of new economic opportunities.

In technological societies, however, redistribution has taken the form of urbanization, which facilitates functional specialization and provides for economies of scale (Davis, 1965). The redistribution has been motivated more by the decline in relative economic health of the rural areas, resulting from labor displaced by mechanization, than by threats to the ecosystem stability of these areas. In the United States, urbanization continues to increase concentration of population in large metropolitan areas as a consequence of migration from smaller cities and towns as well as from rural areas.

The urbanization phenomenon in the United States is characterized by geographic expansion of the city. The dynamics of redistribution involve the centripetal pull of activities and population into urban areas as well as the centrifugal growth of the activities and population in an ever-expanding microregion, the city to megalopolis. The lower-level variables of population distribution consist of the forces behind migration within and immigration into the United States. This dynamic phenomenon is further complicated by its interaction with the other leverage variables—population size, resource consumption, and technology.

Urbanization has generated a host of problems which form part of what is labeled the "urban crisis." The nature and severity of this crisis is a matter of reality and value judgments. The problems are defined by the distance between what is desired and considered as good and what the present situation looks like or is expected to look like sometime in the near future. Of concern to us is the fact that these reality and value judgments are quite limited in perspective. Consequently, the dimensions of the impact space are too narrow to allow the synoptic or comprehensive policy planning that can control the impacts of the population distribution leverage variable throughout the total ecosystem.

Present population distribution patterns in the United States have resulted from economic and technological forces that have developed, in this respect at least, quite free from purposeful policy controls. Whatever government policies relevant to population distribution that exist are fragmented in nature, incremental in application, and frequently work at cross purposes with each other. Government actions and other government policies, however, have significantly, though somewhat inadvertently, affected population distribution. The location of defense facilities in the Southwest and the development of the interstate highway system profoundly affected both interregional and intrametropolitan population redistribution. These actions and policies have been applied without concern for population distribution goals or regard for desirable future population distribution patterns.

Recently, attempts to initiate debate on a comprehensive national urban growth policy have emerged. In fact, when the term "national growth policy" is used among federal agencies, it applies mainly to policy affecting future population distribution and ignores policies affecting population size, resource consumption, and technology, and their synergistic interactions. Even on population distribution, something less than a comprehensive approach is usually taken in the proposed policies. Instead, their strategies for urban growth consider only incremental changes in present patterns—new towns or satellite cities to absorb part of the increased population, for instance (Advisory Commission on Intergovernmental Relations, *Urban and Rural America: Policies for Future Growth*, 1968). The 1970 New Communities Act provides federal loan guarantee and other assistance to new community development by the private sector, with no explicit population distribution goals stated.

In this situation the ecosystem approach becomes extremely valuable for generating new policies. The present policy space for population distribution policy making is too limited. The reality judgments as to the effects of the population distribution variable do not perceive the impacts on linkages throughout every subsystem of the ecosphere. The consequences in terms of intensification of the world macroproblem are far-reaching and long-term. Policy research on population distribution must identify the basic issues involved, challenge the core values and assumptions, and analyze the impacts on the ecosystem of this variable. This research, then, will expand the policy space so that new policies can be generated.

The present policy space for population distribution policy planning is constrained by several assumptions about the nature of the problem and the form of effective policy planning. First of all, present approaches hold that problems associated with population distribution can be disaggregated meaningfully. Thus, specific policies separately address quite isolated factors in urban problems, rural problems, and regional problems. This is the disjointed incremental approach we question at some length in chapter 6, and against which we propose a macrosystem approach that places problems and goals in an ecosystem perspective and optimizes on the basis of the total system in order to plan policy for a desirable alternative future.

The macrosystem approach also challenges the assumption that there are two distinct sets of problems not closely related in causation—socioeconomic problems and environmental problems. Furthermore, the approach would question the value judgment that socioeconomic problems take precedence over environmental problems, especially when it comes to allocation of resources. A macrosystem approach instead relates these two sets of problems and suggests that not only are they amenable to joint solutions but in fact only these joint solutions are optimal.

The above challenges to the prevailing assumptions would suggest that the location of future federal facilities —plants, bases, airports, and highways—should be determined not so much from the standpoint of equalizing economic development as from the standpoint of relieving environmental "hot spots" on a long-term basis. They would also suggest more serious consideration of independently standing new towns, although they are economically less viable than satellite cities (Downs, 1970). Moreover, large construction projects for an economically depressed area would defeat their ultimate purpose if they should destroy the local environment—a healthy environment is essential to any sustained long-term prosperity.

Implementation of the macrosystem approach, furthermore, requires the negation of two currently held assumptions. Policy makers assume that comprehensive goals requiring large-scale population redistribution conflict with deeply held personal values of freedom of choice and resistance to government coercion. These val-

ues actually can provide the basis for comprehensive policy planning in this area. In addition, policy makers
assume that rigidities in existing institutional and governmental structures instrumentally make the population distribution variable unmalleable. At present such
rigidities are part of the macroproblem. There are encouraging signs, however, for improved pliability of institutions in the future.

Therefore, of first-order significance in policy research is the critical need to challenge the core assumptions of policy makers. Once the policy space has been
thus enlarged, specific new alternative policies can be
generated. The potential impacts of these policies can
then be projected in order to assess the effectiveness of
the policies in achieving alternative goals. Policy planning first must perceive population distribution as part of
overall social system behavior and then perceive this behavior as related to the behavior of the ecosystem.

This approach permits consideration of new policy
alternatives, because it recognizes that both the severe
environmental impacts of urbanization and the severe social impacts may be fundamentally related to similar causal factors. It also can refute the objection often raised to
comprehensive distributional policies that the policies involve coercion of individuals. Actually, comprehensive
collective action enlarges the range of desirable futures
about which democratic choices can be made. More instrumentally, collective action resists exogenous economic
and technological forces that, in the absence of such action, dominate population movements. The Commission
on Population Growth and the American Future (1972),
for example, concluded that significant numbers of persons would prefer to live in small or medium-sized cities
but are forced by economic conditions to dwell in large

urban concentrations. Thus, the avoidance of comprehensive planning under the name of freedom of choice ironically has limited freedom of choice.

The systems approach also permits an image of the urban area as a microenvironment. That is, an urban area may be considered as the principal focus of production and consumption—a resource processing (metabolic) activity. The flows of natural and human resources into the city and of the wastes generated, both natural (pollution) and human (unemployment, social instability, etc.), can be monitored. This image of the city as a metabolic process needs to be explored in future research (Wolman, 1965; Ayres, 1972).

In general, these enlarged images of population distribution and urbanization problems enable decision makers to monitor interdependencies, recognizing that policy actions in one subsystem (say, on technological assessment) have important ramifications and second-order effects in others. In addition, the ecosystem image encourages decision makers to recognize that urbanization involves environmental as well as socioeconomic problems. "Overurbanization" causes severe environmental degradation as well as severe socioeconomic problems. Furthermore, the impacts of urbanization are not limited to the local urban and regional environments; the impact space includes national and global resource environments.

For example, urbanization in Southern California has generated national environmental problems as well as local ones. To accommodate this urbanization, water is diverted from Northern California and energy imported from power plants built in the distant areas in the Southwest. In effect, Los Angeles is exporting its pollution to the previously pollution-free Four Corners area and endangering the stability of the ecosystem throughout the Colorado River's hydrological linkages in the United States and Mexico. While this problem is being recognized, few have suggested the consideration of policies that would slow down the urbanization of Los Angeles.

Once policy research has enlarged the dimensions of the policy space and realized the dimensions of the impact space, then alternative macrosystem futures can be postulated. By way of illustration, we suggest four patterns for population distribution to use as alternative societal goals for policy planning:

1. Concentration of population in large metropolitan areas, with characteristic centripetal pull of activities from the entire nation into the urban area and centrifugal growth of those activities out into the geographically-expanding urban region.

2. Concentration of population in large urban areas (as in 1), but with centrifugal growth channeled into satellite cities on the urban periphery.

3. Distribution of population in new growth centers, with the pull of large urban areas countered by these new growth poles established in rural or semiurbanized regions of the country.

4. Diffusion of population throughout rural areas, with people to return to an agrarian or some other kind of nonurban style of life (see *Blueprint for Survival*, 1972).

If policy makers are to choose among these four alternative futures, policy research must calculate and classify the impacts of these alternative patterns. The technological support system exploits the ecosystem-environment in order to produce the goods and services necessary to maintain the population. Therefore, assessment of the environmental impacts of the alternatives must be preceded by a description of the technological support systems necessary to maintain the distribution patterns. This assessment should consider synergic and even the synergistic effects of various technological subsystems as well as consider alternative technologies that would be least disruptive of the ecosystem (most environmentally compatible) while still maintaining the same population distribution.

In addition, research must determine the kinds and levels of resource consumption (i.e., the material standards of living) and the distribution of wealth permitted by the population distribution patterns. Further investigation would explore basic issues and policy mechanisms. Research must determine the institutional and political mechanisms necessary to organize and coordinate the systems as well as their policy-making environments. Finally, it must examine the constraints imposed by social value preferences. Each alternative pattern will require, as well as create, a new life style and value image.

On the basis of this research policy, planning then must make strategic determinations. First, it must ask how much the ecosystem can tolerate in the long run. These ecological limits must then constrain the plans for the rest of the system since survival of the species is the ultimate goal. Second, it must maximize social welfare within the constraints set by the ecosystem. These two steps depend on the clarity with which the ecological limits can be set, but unfortunately present knowledge does not permit an accurate description of many ecological constraints. Thus, policy makers tend to avoid difficult social choices by running ecological risks, pleading uncertainty about the nature and location of the constraints. The macrosystem approach, in contrast, would consciously include the ecological risks and would force policy makers to make choices or broad tradeoffs.

Let us examine further the assumptions that underlie the choice of each of the four alternative patterns of population distribution. Alternatives 1 and 2 are suggested by research (e.g., W. Thompson, *Preface to Urban Economics*, 1965), which indicates that greater amounts of economic production require larger concentrations of population due to economies of scale, specialization of productive activity, and so forth. Preliminary evidence, however, suggests that such concentrations of population are suitable only if ecological limits are estimated liberally and if the value preferences of the society indicate that a high level of economic production is a primary goal. These preferences would imply that the benefits of high level of production outweigh the consequent concentration of political and social power, which would limit individual freedom. Alternatives 3 and 4, in contrast, with decentralization of population, assume that economic activity is reduced in scale, safe ecological limits are estimated, and that individual freedom is to be desired and achieved through elimination of the necessity for high level collective decision making (see Buchanan and Tullock, 1965, for a discussion of determinants of the transfer of decision making to high levels).

Alternative 4 assumes a situation in which ecological limits have been estimated conservatively. It also assumes significantly lower levels of economic activity, as well as significantly higher levels of individual freedom and of participation in the collective decision-making process. With individuals living in small, self-sufficient communities, the actions of one community are least likely to create significant external costs for other communities. Therefore, decision making need not be transferred to high level authorities. In this alternative pattern, significant degrees of individual freedom and small group freedom are achieved at the sacrifice of higher levels of economic activity.

This discussion, then, suggests that explicit attention be given to the pattern of population distribution as an important variable in the impact of the hominisphere on the ecosystem. Policy makers should recognize that efficient exploitation of the environment is related to the manner by which population is distributed. The subsequent distribution of productive activity significantly determines the form of increased economic production. Increased economic activity has costs, however, including instability engendered in the ecosystem as well as social problems associated with urbanization. This expansion of the impact space due to recognition of the population distribution variable thus encourages an expansion of the policy space. Such expansion generates decentralized population distribution patterns as alternatives consistent with conservatively estimated ecological limits, reduction in social instability, and enhancement of individual freedom.

Policy on Resource Consumption

The resource consumption leverage variable describes the extent to which the hominisphere draws from the rest of the ecosystem for support of man's activities. When considered jointly with population size, it is often useful to think of resource consumption on a per capita, or average per person, basis.

Since the per capita resource consumption generally goes hand in hand with per capita gross national product (GNP), the two have been used interchangeably in general discussions about the environmental impact of human activities. From an ecosystem viewpoint, however, it will be important to distinguish between the two, and it will be preferable to use per capita resource consumption as the leverage variable. This is because resource consumption and GNP are not always directly proportional. After a society achieves a certain level of affluence, such as in the United States, resource consumption tends to increase less rapidly than GNP. With appropriate policies, this discrepancy can be made even more pronounced. A crude explanation is that GNP consists of both goods and services. As there is usually less resource consumption in the production of services than in the production of goods, the shift toward a service-dominated economy in a postindustrial society uses proportionately less resources as GNP continues to increase.

A proportionate decrease, of course, does not imply an absolute decrease. Therefore, patterns of consumption of both goods and services should be carefully studied. Certain services (e.g., foreign travel) consume a great deal more resources from the ecosystem than other services (e.g., enjoyment of performing arts). Furthermore, the service industries draw from goods industries (e.g., accounting use of electronic computers), and vice versa (e.g., automobiles' need for repair services). Similarly, if growth is to be the tool for reducing poverty, lower-income groups will first increase their consumption of goods before making large demands on the service sectors. Thus, from the ecosystem viewpoint, it will be desirable to focus on resource consumption as the leverage variable. This focus allows the possibility of unabated economic growth measured in GNP with a stable or curtailed rate of resource consumption.

Consideration of specific policies on resource consumption (e.g., import of petroleum) leads to consideration of lower-level variables in terms of consumption of specific foods, minerals, and fuels. Actual consumption, of course, depends on the demand and supply, the resulting price, and the substitutability of each resource. From the ecosystem viewpoint, however, resources are seldom really consumed; they are only transformed physically or chemically. Minerals in particular are not destroyed in the process of resource consumption; they are only diluted or disordered in the process. Theoretically, they can be recovered to a usable state by recycling. Recycling, however, takes energy and organization. So does mining, and increasingly so as we either dig deeper for high-grade ores or process easily obtained low-grade ores. From this viewpoint, we may consider that our world contains a vast, stored thermodynamic potential and that "the two essential forms of stored potential are energy and order" (Berry, 1972, p. 8). This concept can lead to a reliable and precise index for resource consumption from the ecosystem viewpoint, although much further development of the concept is needed to make such an index as useful for policy decisions as GNP has been.

Both past and current United States policies on resource consumption have been anchored on the prevailing economic beliefs of the American society. Thus they assume that the most efficient use of resources will result if the effective decisions are made in the marketplace. The guiding principle has been the reliance on the free, laissez-faire market economy based on competition, usually modified by government interference only when deemed absolutely necessary. The interlocking assumptions or corollaries are that competition stimulates technological development and, therefore, that scarcity of any resource will be circumvented via technological substitution by another resource. To the extent that the chain of substitution can continue indefinitely, resources are inexhaustible and the exponentially growing demand for materials and energy can and should always be satisfied.

In practice, this guiding principle has never been strictly followed. While some economists blame many social and economic problems on the failure to abide by the principle of a free and competitive economy, most economists try to explain why the principle is now too idealistic for society to follow. First of all, the condition of perfect competition, on which the principle is predicated, is very seldom approached in our economic system as it has evolved. Technology alone, with its resultant economy of scale, tends to encourage oligopoly, if not monopoly. Other factors, such as imperfect information, tend to destroy perfect competition and invite government regulation. Theoretically, the free economy and its accompanying price system does not lead to an equalized distribution of income and wealth, a condition increasingly demanded for social justice and which also requires government action. Then, too, interest groups and large corporate organizations frequently demand government interference with the free market in spite of their conservative philosophy. For example, they ask for government restriction of imports, pleading the excuses of national security and economic injury. During economic recessions, government expenditure to generate demand is generally accepted as a desirable pump-priming device.

From the ecosystem viewpoint, the "modified" free market economy is not much different from a purely free market economy. In either instance, the economy is locked in a path of growing resource consumption. During economic booms, private corporations both react to and generate increasing demand by advertisement, designed obsolescence, and so forth. During economic recessions, governments keep the demand up by initiating public-work projects, accelerating construction of government facilities, etc. "The psychology of more" (Looft, 1971), the growth ethic, the measurement of "quality of life" in materialistic terms, the spiral of wage and price increases, and the social goal of full employment all work together to keep the growth going. The first serious challenge, or threat of challenge, to this trend came only recently with the environmental movement.

The historical background of the current and forceful environmental movement deserves mention. In spite of the operational dominance in national economic growth of the belief that the most efficient use of resources emanates from effective decisions in the marketplace, real concern over impacts of resource limitations has a history of more than a century in the United States (Allen, 1959, pp. 8 ff). This concern became a bona fide conservation movement about 1907 during the administration of one of its champions, President Theodore Roosevelt, and led to the 1909 inter-American conference on natural resource questions. By 1946, global concern over the emerging problems was registered in the United Nations Scientific Conference on the Conservation and Utilization of Natural Resources held at Lake Success for the enlightenment of international statesmen. The 1972 United Nations Conference on the Human Environment, held in Stockholm, is a climax to an era since the end of World War II of evolution from primary involvement of governmental agencies and professional conservationists to widespread public concern and rise of value-laden environmentalism. Meanwhile, the definition of conservation as wise use of natural resources, rather than preservation, has been progressively reinforced.

The challenge to the economy of growth from the

forceful environmental movement of today has thus come in two steps: first, refocusing attention on the hazards to primary linkages in the ecosystem caused by the increase in pollutants generated in the process of growth, and second, bringing many people to concern themselves with the ultimate limits to resource consumption.

Most economists tend to respond to the first challenge on the basis of their concept of externality. When side effects are generated in a production or consumption process, such as the unintentional generation of pollution, "external economies and diseconomies" result, and the market mechanism alone may not produce the best allocation of resources. There are at least four ways of dealing with such externality (Turvey, 1966):

Regulation by public authorities, e.g., prohibiting the use of certain fuels or requiring that effluents be treated in accordance with certain standards;

Contract between the party that causes and the party that is subject to external effects, usually with payments by one to the other resulting in maximum total gain or minimum total loss;

Taxes imposed by the public authorities at a rate supposedly commensurate to the external diseconomy, or excess of social cost over private cost; and

Centralizing decision making for the group of units whose activities have external effects on each other.

These four ways differ in their degrees of trying to "internalize the externalities" and in their pros and cons. "Effluent charges," a form of taxes on effluents, have the advantage of permitting each polluter to find his "least-cost mix," for example, by joining hands to realize certain economies of scale in large-scale treatment facilities, thereby minimizing the total cost of cleaning up a river (Rose, 1970). In contrast, regulations are easy to police and are simple for the public to understand and use to put legal and moral pressure on polluters. The choice of the most appropriate way thus depends on the specific local situation.

In the last few years, the federal government, especially with the Environmental Protection Agency, has used a policy mix of these four ways to try to combat pollution generated in the private sector. Notable examples are the regulations regarding the use of high-sulfur fuels, the use of DDT, and the emission standards for future automobiles. Similar if not more stringent policy has been applied to the public sector. For example, the National Environmental Policy Act of 1969 stipulates:

> All agencies of the federal government shall . . . include in every recommendation or report on proposals for legislation and other major federal actions significantly affecting the quality of the human environment, a detailed statement by the responsible official on—
> (i) the environmental impact of the proposed action;
> (ii) any adverse environmental effects which cannot be avoided should the proposal be implemented;
> (iii) alternatives to the proposed action;
> (iv) the relationship between local short-term uses of man's environment and the maintenance and enhancement of long-term productivity; and
> (v) any irreversible and irretrievable commitments

of resources which would be involved in the proposed action should it be implemented.

Prior to making any detailed statement, the responsible federal official shall consult with and obtain the comments of any federal agency which has jurisdiction by law or special expertise with respect to any environmental impact involved (p. 269).

The above measures for environmental protection have had an indirect effect on resource consumption. The internalized cost of externalities has generally been passed on by the producer to the consumer. To the extent that demand decreases with increasing price, the resource consumption has decreased with demand. The basic forces behind growth, however, have not changed fundamentally. Judging from the statistics on energy and mineral demand, there is no noticeable abatement in the exponential growth of resource consumption. The major reaction seems to have come mainly from the producers who have been directly affected by the regulations. In some cases the growth ethic has even been successfully used as a tool to reduce or postpone regulation via implicit and explicit threats of higher prices and lost jobs.

The second challenge, the environmentalists' concern for the ultimate limit to resource consumption, in contrast to the first, has caused heated debate because it poses a direct challenge to growth. From the ecosystem viewpoint, unabated growth in resource consumption will reach limits sooner or later; the only question is when and where. The "thermodynamic potential" concept establishes a major limit difficult to avoid on the waste heat associated with our total energy consumption. When this limit will be reached is uncertain, because it depends on technological and institutional responses and because we still know very little about the capacity of the earth to sustain higher temperatures without disrupting the primary linkages of our ecosystem. Reaching this limit might be postponed if we design our environment as a total system so that the waste heat is used to advantage, if we learn how better to use solar, geothermal, wind, and tidal energy, if we learn how to dissipate heat more efficiently into outer space, and if we disperse population concentrations in order to avoid local hot spots. Some estimates have indicated, however, that the limit may be only 50 years away and in certain urban areas it may be as close as 25 years (Tsongas, et al., 1970). This environmental limit, acting in concert with the demand for reliable and clean energy in the immediate future, and with the rapid depletion of fossil fuels as well as many high-grade mineral ores, has convinced many people of the need to adopt an ecosystemic image in their judgments of reality.

If we take a global ecosystem view, as Boulding does, then "the essential measure of the success of the economy is not production and consumption (GNP), but the nature, extent, quality, and complexity of the total capital stock, including in this the state of the human bodies and minds included in the system" (Boulding, 1966). In such an economy, stock of resources is more important than resource consumption, or flow of resources. One might even conceive a stationary-state economy (Daly, 1971, pp. 231–32) in which the flow of resources will have leveled off from the current exponential growth. Daly describes the stationary state as "a constant stock of physical wealth (capital) and a constant stock of people (population)." Within this constant stock, a high rate of throughput (production) is at some point ecologically "impracticable"; instead, our goal should be a rate of throughput "as low as possible," since it is really the cost of maintaining the stock. Limits on the size and through-put of stock must be determined on the basis of ecological constraints and technological capabilities. Unfortunately, determining the distribution of stock is not easy to envis-age; it may be, as Daly suggests, the most difficult aspect of any proposed transition to a stationary-state economy:

> For several reasons the important issue of the sta-tionary state will be distribution, not production. The problem of relative shares can no longer be avoided by appeals to growth. The argument that everyone should be happy as long as his absolute share of the wealth increases, regardless of his rela-tive share, will no longer be available. Absolute and relative shares will move together, and the division of physical wealth will be a zero sum game. Also the arguments justifying inequality in wealth as neces-sary for savings, investment, and growth will lose their force. With production flows (which are really *costs* of maintaining the stock) kept low, the focus will be on the distribution of the stock of wealth, not on the distribution of the flow of income. Marginal productivity theories and "justifications" pertain only to flows and therefore are not available to explain or "justify" the distribution of stock ownership. It is hard to see how ethical appeals to equal shares can be countered. Also, even though physical stocks re-main constant, increased income in the form of lei-sure will result from continued technological im-provements. How will it be distributed, if not according to some ethical norm of equality? The sta-tionary state would make fewer demands on our en-vironmental resources, but much greater demands on our moral resources (Daly, p. 237).

Again, however, we point out that a stationary or steady-state economy can very well have unabated growth of GNP but a stable rate of resource consumption as measured perhaps by a constant annual decrease of "thermodynamic potential" indicator.

If one accepts the stationary-state economy for serious consideration as a possible alternative future, it will not be difficult to generate new policies on resource consumption to encourage progress toward this economy. With respect to energy, a recent report sponsored by the Office of Science and Technology (1970, p. xi) stated:

> It would . . . involve an examination of pricing policies, rate structures, advertising programs, tax policies, and other factors in the economy affecting growth. . . . It may well be timely to re-examine all of the basic factors that shape the present rapid rate of energy growth in the light of our resource base and the impact of growth on the environment.

Such an examination would generate many available alternative policies to encourage thrift in energy usage, for example, the use of an inverse rate structure which charges more for additional electrical units rather than less. Unlike the present rate structure, such a structure, which has been used in Europe, would penalize heavy users rather than light users. Other noneconomic policies could encourage building designs and locations which did not require massive air-conditioning and/or heating and technological innovations in the use of "waste" heat and improved insulation. The goal of increased efficiency in the use of energy could be applied in all areas of production, consumption, and disposal, from light bulbs to aluminum cans to massive machinery.

Other policies can be generated to encourage steady

"flow" of resources. For example, regulations could be put on "durable goods" to make them really durable by stipulating that they pass certain minimum life-cycle tests. When the federal government tries to stimulate economic development in depressed areas or during depressed periods, it could create public-sector work in human services, which are low in resource consumption, rather than in construction projects with high material requirements. For transportation systems, the emphasis could be given to mass transit and bicycle paths rather than to highways.

Although the concept of a steady-state economy has attracted support from certain parts of the business circle (Peceei, 1971) and has found its way into U.S. Senate debate (Committee on Interior and Insular Affairs, 1971), it has drawn heavy fire from both establishment and radical economists. (It is interesting to note that when economists begin seriously to question the value of growth, at least some of their colleagues no longer view them as economists but, instead, as in the instance of Kenneth Boulding, as ecologists [Heller, 1971, p. 21].) In general, these arguments in support of economic growth fall into five broad categories.

Perhaps the most abstract of these arguments centers around the issue of progress. Looft, in a discussion of *Nature, Man and Woman* by Alan Watts, suggests that "Western cultures are 'progressive and historical', characterized by the prevailing philosophy that human society is on the move, that the political state is an organism destined to grow and expand." In a materialistically oriented society, such as our own, economic growth is viewed as the main form of progress and, therefore, by implication, an economics of equilibrium is viewed as stagnating and anti-evolutionary. In contrast, he describes Eastern cultures "as 'traditional and nonhistorical'. These societies do not see themselves to be in linear movement toward temporal goals" (Looft, 1971, pp. 563–64).

The second type of progrowth argument purports to take a global view by suggesting that economic growth is essential for maintaining the political and military power of the United States in its dealings with other nations (Knorr, 1961, pp. 9–18). In a world of scarcity this argument is based on an expectation of future resource shortage. This "global view" does not transcend the hominisphere perspective.

The third type of progrowth argument deals with distribution of wealth and, in general, is based on the assumption that a significant redistribution of wealth is either politically impossible or economically inadequate (Slichter, 1961, p. 19). Growth is seen as the only politically feasible method to increase the absolute income of the poor and thereby eliminate poverty. Similarly, growth is seen as necessary for providing the economic resources needed to solve the problems of the cities, education, social security, medical care, etc. (Heller, 1971, p. 11). To curtail growth in resource consumption will cost many jobs in the short run, push the cost of energy and basic goods up, and thereby hit the poor the hardest. Progrowth and antigrowth advocates agree on this point; they merely disagree on the solution, i.e., growth versus redistribution. On an international scale the progrowth advocates assume that the United States will not radically shift its priorities by providing a significantly larger percentage of its budget for foreign aid to the less-developed countries. To increase aid to these countries, therefore, requires economic growth to increase the size of our budget base (Knorr, 1961, p. 11).

The fourth and fifth types of progrowth arguments center on environmental and natural resource issues. Argument four is quite similar to the third argument in suggesting that additional revenues from growth are needed to pay the costs of cleaning up the environment and recycling natural resources (Heller, 1971, pp. 11, 13, 14; Crocker, 1971, pp. 13, 14). Progrowth economists explain, using a simple supply-and-demand curve, that the increased costs of production associated with pollution abatement equipment and the increased costs associated with the disposal and recycling of residuals will serve to shift current supply curves to the left, driving prices up and reducing consumption. At the same time, through economic growth it will be possible to increase per capita income and thereby shift current demand curves to the right. In other words, we could afford to absorb the increase in prices while actually maintaining or even increasing current levels of production and consumption.

In a similar vein, growth is asserted to be necessary for creating an economic environment which will encourage research and risk-taking in innovative methods of solving current problems (Heller, 1971, p. 13; Crocker, 1971, pp. 13, 14). By nurturing this type of economic environment and by encouraging the application of "high technology" to societal problems—as does President Nixon's Technology Opportunities Program announced in 1972—we could solve many of our environmental and resource problems without significant leftward shifts in supply curves. Since many of these problems seem to be growing at a faster rate than the economy, the implicit premise in this argument is that large doses of technology will actually shift the supply curves associated with our problem solutions to the right. This argument is in contrast to that of Hardin (1968, p. 1243) and others, who argue that many of our most pressing social problems have no technical solutions.

The fifth type of progrowth argument asks the question: What happens if we stop growing? What happens if the supply curve (or demand curve) takes that fateful shift to the left? The answer is not too palatable, and is explained in part by what is called the "acceleration principle" (Samuelson, 1961). This principle is an important element in the expansions and contractions of the business cycle. Based on the acceleration principle, an economist can predict that a reduction or even a leveling off in the growth rate will have a significant effect upon the capital goods sector, which in turn will have a significant negative effect on the consumption goods sector. In other words, a reduction in growth will lead to unemployment, which will feed upon itself to cause further unemployment. In the midst of such a recession or depression, a growth advocate would point out that there would be no way to solve environmental, resource, and social problems. As a corollary, an economist would mention that growth also will be necessary to provide wage employment for an increasing population. To increase or even maintain current levels of per capita income will require economic growth to exceed population growth.

How are we to judge the merits of the complex arguments for and against growth? The intensity and emotionalism with which the issues are debated indicate that no methodologies or criteria have yet been agreed upon. It might, therefore, be helpful to suggest a few appropriate criteria for judging the merits of growth. Since the growth ethic would have to be considered the dominant paradigm at present, these criteria will indicate the conditions for a successful argument against the concept of growth in resource consumption.

The first criterion which would indicate a negative effect of growth is one which many critics claim has already been documented. It would require that economic growth be shown to actually worsen the distribution of wealth. That this might be the case was recently indicated by Cambridge Institute researchers, who found that the average gap (calculated in 1970 dollars) between the poorest one-fifth and the wealthiest one-fifth of the persons in the United States was $13,729 in 1958 and $18,888 in 1968 (Wicker, 1972). This, of course, does not mean that the absolute position of the lowest fifth has not improved.

On a more abstract level, growth would be seriously questioned if it could be shown to threaten democratic principles or current human values. For instance, large-scale systems and bureaucracies, which tend to be associated with growth, might be demonstrated to be unresponsive to individual inputs, to increase alienation, and so forth. Similarly, growth could be successfully challenged if the organizational structures, technologies, degree of specialization, and population distributions required for growth were shown to be inherently unstable and maladaptive (Rappaport, 1971). Ecologists increasingly make this charge with respect to monoculture farming and heavy pesticide usage of large agrobusiness industries (Ehrlich, 1970; Horsfall, 1970). The distribution problems associated with thermal "hot spots" and the overloading of local environments would also fit into this category.

In the area of resource depletion, growth would be effectively challenged if recycling of residuals could be shown to be of limited applicability. Growth in the developed countries, especially, would then be viewed as fulfilling artificial needs while wasting valuable resources. At least in the near future, diminishing returns, energy shortages, and the law of entropy should all apply to recycling. It would therefore seem that such a case could be made. If so, a transition from an economy based on planned obsolescence to one based on durability (Boulding, 1966; Daly, 1971) would be an important objective.

With respect to the environment, growth would be challenged if the marginal costs could be shown to exceed the marginal benefits; that is, if the increased generation of pollution or toxic materials associated with an increase in production could be shown to exceed the capacity of the pollution absorption equipment purchased with the increased revenue from growth. At this point in time, it is difficult to predict whether the long-range benefits of growth will be able to keep pace with the costs. The answers will come from current and future research on the tolerance of the environment to various pollution levels as well as on the ability of technological innovation to compensate for diminishing returns.

The final criterion is also the most interesting. Economic growth as a policy for social and environmental progress would be successfully challenged if it could be shown that events and circumstances in the physical and social environment will combine to make growth (on the scale required) impossible to achieve. This would imply that a different strategy for the solution of our problems would be in order. Such challenge might come from either of two directions. First, an analysis might show the costs of the needed solutions to exceed the available revenues from even the most optimistic growth projections. Or, second, an analysis might show current or expected trends to tend to depress growth. Such an assessment of growth potential would consider the effects of resource shortages, costs of internalizing externalities, costs of recycling, costs of increased monitoring and regulation, demands for increased equity in wages (equal pay for women), changing values (antimaterialism and equity with less-developed nations), inflation, uncertainties, international monetary and political crises, diminishing returns, breakdowns in social and technological support systems, increased demands for leisure, and so forth. The "acceleration principle," mentioned earlier, could suggest that the combined effects of these economic depressants would not have to be extreme to create a downward spiral in which growth would be excessively costly if not impossible. Under such conditions the pursuit of growth would be an improper strategy for solving social and environmental problems. The argument then would be, if transition to a stationary economy is inevitable, then we should develop policies to ease rather than impede the transition.

The intention here has not been to suggest that a stationary economy is the solution to our environmental and resource problems, nor that all forms of economic growth are undesirable. As noted earlier, stationary resource consumption is not the same as stationary GNP. We have, instead, tried to review and summarize many of the basic issues, assumptions, and alternatives involved in an ongoing, and increasingly noisy, debate over the efficacy of the growth ethic—a debate whose outcome will not be known for many years to come. Perhaps the most that can be said today is any outcome will require enormous institutional, structural, and value changes to adjust to the limits of a finite world. The adoption of policies congruent with stationary resource consumption will depend on the reality judgments of policy makers as to how far we are from these ultimate limits. In the short run, the prevailing policies of merely internalizing externalities can serve useful purposes. But in the long run, rational

policies on resource consumption and environmental degradation can be generated and deliberated only after reliable and precise ecosystemic indicators of environmental
and resource conditions have been developed to be as operational for policy decisions of the future as GNP has
been in the past.

Policy on Technology

Technology has been defined both broadly and narrowly.
For example, technology can refer only to knowledge
used for the construction of machines or hardware. More
broadly, it can include the application of knowledge in
the three categories of engineering processes for materials, energy, and information. Most comprehensively, it includes all of man's knowledge for manipulating anything
within the ecosystem. The following definition (Mesthene, 1970, p. 25) is a compromise useful for present purposes:

> Technology is the organization of knowledge for the
> achievement of practical ends. As such, it includes
> not only machines, but also intellectual tools such as
> computer languages and contemporary analytical
> and mathematical techniques.

This inclusion of social technology renders quite artificial
the distinction between technologies that involve physical
objects and those that involve organizations. To many
persons the pervasive influence of technology in society
creates an image of a "techno-social" response. A techno-
social response or solution, in this context, is any technological development, including software and analytical
techniques, accompanied by some corresponding social
enterprise or change (Schwartz, 1971).

Techno-social responses currently are held in high

esteem by policy makers, as was noted in the discussion on resource consumption and economic systems. Such responses to problems however, often avoid their underlying causes because the technological "solution" often is based on an inadequate reality image. The ecosystem image of reality quickly establishes physical limits that many persons who embraced technology heretofore have not accepted. To accept the ecosystem image they would have to adjust their values and images significantly.

Many persons now view attempts at technological circumvention of physical limits and environmental constraints as a manly and worthy challenge. They hail the first step on the moon as a "giant step for mankind." Successful circumvention reinforces man's ego and is compatible with his anthropocentric view of the world. In addition, the discussion in "Basic Issues" alluded to how technological progress is sanctioned and legitimized by religious heritage. "Modern technology is at least partly to be explained as an Occidental, voluntarist realization of the Christian dogma of man's transcendence of, and rightful mastery over, nature" (White, 1967, p. 1206). Furthermore, technology is an intrinsic part of the Post-Renaissance "rational ideology" (Skolimowski, 1970, p. 21). Consequently, technology is central to the reality image currently held by most decision makers. This image has been reinforced by the dramatic and immediate benefits they perceive technology to bring. Their reality image ignores or diminishes the fact that technological benefits often have hidden or deferred costs.

Although much has been written about technology, its contribution to the formation of the macroproblem requires some attention. Technology has been a stimulus to growth (and vice versa) because of certain attributes that the ecosystem perspective puts into focus.

In addition to easing symptoms without affecting underlying causes, the technological variable often disturbs primary ecosystem linkages. Technology enables man to consume resources more efficiently and to provide for his basic needs—food, shelter, transportation, energy, and water supply. This activity can lead, however, to positive disruption of primary linkages as well as to the weakening of negative feedbacks (limits) on growth of population and capital (see Meadows et al., 1972).

Technology, furthermore, strongly affects population distribution and social organization, as was discussed above. Mesthene (1970, p. 65) points out that technological development requires increasingly more complex social institutions—cities, corporations, universities, and government—which lead to increased centralization of authority. Conversely, decentralized distribution of persons in certain instances is strongly dependent on technological systems. The dispersal or migration of the United States population to the arid Southwest, for example, relies heavily on engineered water supply, transportation, and electrical power networks.

Another attribute of technology, as Brooks points out (Brooks, 1972, p. 1), is that it substitutes algorithms for human judgment and can be reproduced by relatively unskilled persons working in hierarchical organizations. A good example is the automobile production-assembly line.

There has been no explicit United States policy on science and technology. The traditional American faith in science as the means for human progress has taken on sobering sophistication. Since World War II, the increasing support by the federal government for research and development, especially in the applied areas of defense, space, health, and agriculture, has created a complex of interlocking estates—the scientific, the professional, the administrative, and the political (Price, 1965). The inward growth of this complex in terms of the mutual defenses of the estates, and its outward growth in terms of the size and impact of its activities have led to certain core assumptions frequently espoused by policy makers when they make decisions related to technology. For example, they frequently assume that most problems have a technological solution. In addition, they assume any problems created by technology can be corrected by more technology. This implies that corrective measures can be instituted in time as problems arise, and that any unwanted side effects or second-order consequences of technological development can be prevented or mitigated by "technology assessment." Some policy makers even consider the traditional market mechanism a satisfactory procedure for stimulating technological development in directions of providing new, socially desirable public goods and services. Others assume that, with the massive support of the federal government for research and development, technological development cannot but serve the "public interest."

This technological *Weltanschauung* has other important features which make it of central concern to us in this study. These features were addressed in general in the section on "Basic Issues," and illustrate some core assumptions that must be challenged before truly new alternative policies can be generated. In one sense technological development is considered a neutral activity—it is not considered to be autonomous or to inculcate (or demand) certain values in society. This assumed feature, however, can be said to conflict with other assumptions held concurrently. So, too, will reductionism or specialization of function, which is often regarded as necessary and harmless in scientific or technological endeavors. In a positive sense, technology is considered to liberate the individual by giving him a greater freedom of choice and action. In a negative sense, many persons hold that we cannot abandon technological progress because of the traumatic socioeconomic dislocations and problems this would cause.°

Such assumptions frequently conflict with those inherent in an ecosystem image. These factors must be kept in mind when considering the impact of technology on population size and the policies for technological circumvention of the problems of growth.

The most significant impact of present technological policy on population size has been to reduce the death rate rather than curb the birth rate. Technology has stimulated rather than stabilized population growth, perhaps inadvertently, and has been applied mainly to cope with problems associated with population growth. For example, technological developments have fostered population growth by providing medicine and public health on the one hand and by increasing food production and water supply on the other.

Even so, technological solutions for curbing excessive rates in human populations do exist and in fact could be further refined. Advanced contraceptive technology is now available, although a system completely free of uncertainty and medical side effects does not yet exist. Methods such as the pill, condoms, and intrauterine devices depend upon voluntary use and have had varying degrees of success. Their feasibility and social acceptance

---

° Technology is considered to be completely rational, not requiring an act of faith. In a working paper, Gray and Mathes (1972) challenge this assumption and point out that, within an image perspective, technology has become a mystique.

differ considerably, depending upon operational considerations and value premises related to the socioeconomic,
ethnic, and religious makeup of the population in which
the methods are made available.

Abortifacients, another distinct technological solution, are not yet at the same stage of development or acceptance as are the contraceptives. Involuntary systems
are also under discussion and are likely to be technically
feasible in the near future. These include compounds put
in drinking water supplies or in common foodstuffs to
prevent conception. Policy analysis with judgmental descriptive elements would show that the social resistance
to this type of birth control technology, for instance,
would render it highly unacceptable in terms of the ecosystemic classification scheme.

From an ecosystem view we know that unlimited
growth of animal and plant populations in nature is not
possible. Their growth is blocked by a number of constraints, such as availability of water and nutrients, space
and light requirements, predation, parasitism, system controls, etc. The more mature and stable an ecosystem, the
more numerous and sophisticated the controls on growth.

Unlimited growth of human populations is also
blocked by similar constraints or negative feedback loops.
These constraints include limitations in food production,
resource availability, resource degradation, crowding,
and limitations in the waste-assimilating capacity of the
natural environment. Human populations, however, cir-
cumvent or relax these constraints by technological developments, together with sociopolitical organization and
response. Together these form techno-social solutions,
usually short-term, to the problems posed by the constraints.

Present policy looks for techno-social solutions to

relax constraints rather than to curb rates of growth and consumption. Planners assume they can find techno-social solutions to most problems. That these same solutions might engender or exacerbate the problems is only now beginning to be considered by a few (for a discussion of these effects with particularly apt examples, see Lagler, 1969). This consideration is a serious and legitimate question for policy debate, and forms the basis of our working hypothesis about techno-social solutions.

Our working hypothesis about the nature of techno-social solutions and the conclusions one might draw from it is adapted from a model proposed by Schwartz (1971, 62–77). This hypothesis can be summarized in stepwise fashion as follows:

1. Because of the interrelationships and limitations existing within a closed system, a techno-social solution is never complete and hence is a quasi solution.
2. Each quasi solution generates a set of "residue" or new techno-social problems arising from (*a*) incompleteness, (*b*) augmentation, and (*c*) secondary effects.
3. The residue problems proliferate faster than solutions can be found to meet them.
4. Each successive set of residue problems is more difficult to solve than predecessor problems because of seven factors:
    a) dynamics of technology
    b) increased complexity
    c) increased cost
    d) decreased resources
    e) growth and expansion
    f) requirements for greater control
    g) inertia of social institutions

5. In the absence of strict technology assessment and policy controls,° residues of unsolved techno-social problems converge in an advanced technological society to a point where techno-social solutions are no longer possible.

To illustrate this hypothesis, the proliferation of residue problems resulting from the application of a single techno-social (or quasi) solution to a problem is shown diagrammatically in figure 13. The differing intensities or complexities of the problems are suggested by the relative size of the circles.

The application of many techno-social solutions to a series of first generation problems gives rise to an extreme proliferation of residue problems known as a residue chain. This proliferation of residue problems in a chain-like manner is shown diagrammatically in figure 14. The relationships between problems can affect the problems in the residue chain in two ways:

1. A residue problem of one quasi solution can cancel or negate the quasi solution of another problem.
2. A residue problem of one quasi solution can reinforce a residue problem of another quasi solution.

This basic concept of a residue problem network can be used to evaluate the impacts of technological developments in a number of problem areas. The areas that should be considered first are those which are critical for the sustenance of human life and in which the technology leverage variable today plays a key role. An ecosystem

° A phrase missing in the original hypothesis. Note that techno-social solutions may still exist for individual problems while no solution exists for the totality of problems. This phenomenon of totality is one aspect of the macroproblem.

image is necessary for this approach. It is evident from the viewpoint of this hypothesis that present technology policy is inadequate because it takes a disjointed incremental approach and fails to get down to basic issues and values.

Stable ecosystems are characterized by well-developed feedback control, low entropy, high information content, high diversity, well organized stratification and spatial heterogeneity, low net community production, closed nutrient cycles, and a high energy input directed toward maintenance of the system as opposed to production. The impacts of modern agricultural technology, to take the example illustrated in figure 14, counter these characteristics. This technology is directed toward high productivity at the cost of stability (Odum, 1969).

Monoculture and simplification of ecosystems practiced in modern agricultural technology encourage outbreaks of pests, which then must be countered with pesticides. The practices also encourage rapid depletion of soil nutrients, which then must be countered by massive applications of fertilizers. These in turn pollute both surface and ground water (Commoner, 1971; Schuphan, 1972). In addition, large crop yields resulting from inorganic fertilizers are not necessarily synonymous with crop quality—for example, the protein content of Kansas wheat has been steadily declining for the past several decades (Albrecht, 1956). Finally, modern large-scale irrigation projects are still plagued with the age-old problem of salinization of the soil from the accumulation of unused salts as residuals from the metabolized or evaporated irrigation water (Stead, 1969; Michel, 1972).

Even the most seemingly benign and well-intentioned technological projects often are fraught with unanticipated and unintended but nevertheless highly dis-

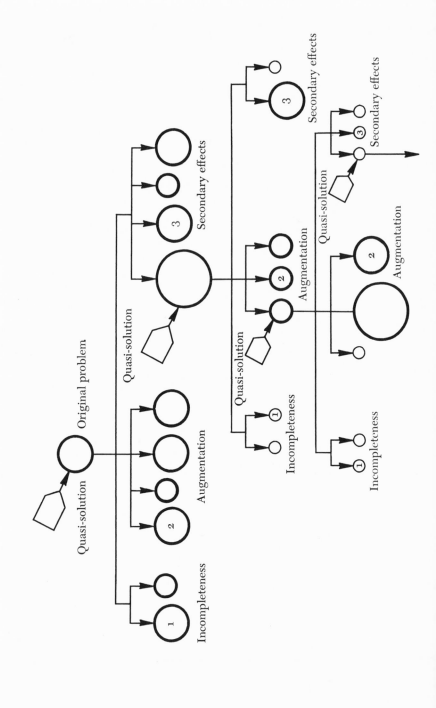

Definitions:

1. Incompleteness—The inability to obtain a complete solution because of restrictions imposed by efficiency limits, size, weight, material, and operational considerations.

2. Augmentation—A jump to a new level of technological achievement and complexity and its attendant requirements as a result of some "breakthrough" solution to a problem.

3. Secondary effects—Indirect and largely unanticipated side effects initiated or caused by a solution to a given problem.

Fig. 13. Three generations of residue problems resulting from application of a techno-social solution to a problem (adapted from Schwartz, 1971, p. 66).

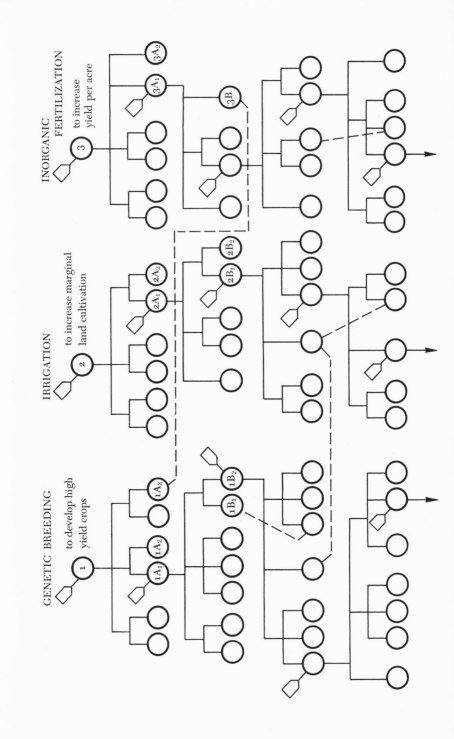

KEY TO RESIDUE CHAIN:

Problem No. 1

Develop High Yield Crops by Genetic Breeding

$1A_1$ Greater energy requirements (tillage, harvesting, etc.)
 Solution: Shift to energy-intensive monoculture
$1A_2$ Greater fertilizer requirements
$1A_3$ Increased vulnerability to blights and diseases
$1B_1$ People displaced from farms
$1B_2$ Monoculture leads to pest outbreaks
 Solution: Pesticides

Problem No. 2

Bring Marginal Lands under Cultivation by Irrigation

$2A_1$ Salinization of soil results
 Solution: Install underdrains and leach soils
$2A_2$ Soil erosion and sedimentation
$2B_1$ Eutrophication of surface waters from leachate
$2B_2$ Nitrate contamination of ground water from leachate

Problem No. 3

Increase Agricultural Yield by Application of Inorganic Fertilizers

$3A_1$ Decrease in protein content and nutritional value of food
 Solution: Chemically fortify food
$3A_2$ Eutrophication of surface waters from fertilizers in run-off
$3B$ Adverse effects on human health

Fig. 14. Partial residue chain analysis based on techno-social solutions to problems of agricultural production (application of Schwartz, 1971, p. 60

ruptive ecological side effects. A virtual litany of such examples is contained in the proceedings of the Conference on Ecological Aspects of International Development convened by the Conservation Foundation and the Center for the Biology of Natural Systems (Farvar and Milton, 1972). A particularly striking example is the introduction of veterinary services in Africa to control the tsetse fly. The tsetse fly had played an important natural role in preventing overgrazing of the savanna ecosystem. Indirectly, tsetse control programs have contributed to degradation of the savanna through the chain of events shown in figure 15.

The lesson is clear. Present policy planning for technological development brings only mixed blessings because of impacts on natural linkages throughout the ecosystem. Various alternatives need to be more carefully considered from an ecosystem view than heretofore. High productivity no longer suffices as the principal criterion by which to judge a technology policy. A policy must be evaluated in terms of its impact on ecosystem stability.

Policy research must demonstrate to policy makers that valid alternatives exist, alternatives which still may be technological. For example, alternative agricultural policies should pay attention to the feasibility of tapping the detritus food chain and of harvesting hardy, disease-resistant vegetation of all types and converting it into edible form by microbial and chemical technologies. A more comprehensive ecosystem alternative would be the compartment model for managing environmental units in which growth type, steady state, and intermediate type ecosystems can be linked with urban and industrial areas for mutual benefit. Knowing the transfer coefficients that define the flow of energy and the movement of materials and organisms (including man) between compartments, it should be possible to determine rational limits for the size and capacity of each compartment (Odum, 1969).

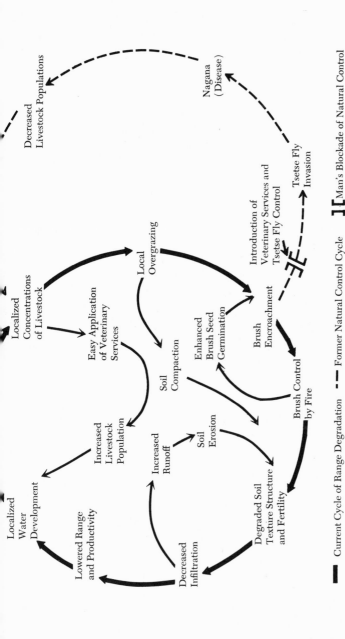

Fig. 15. The effect of man's interference on the savanna ecosystem. Veterinary services, tsetse fly eradication programs, and increased local water supplies have interfered with the natural control of livestock population on the savanna and contributed to problems of overgrazing (*Institute of Ecology Report*, 1972, p. 188).

Such alternatives can be generated as soon as the macrosystem approach enables us systematically to challenge the core assumptions behind current technology policy. One core assumption is that we cannot abandon technological progress because of the traumatic dislocations and problems this would cause. The validity of this assumption hinges on what we mean by "technological progress," because it should already be evident that technologies can differ considerably in their focus and attributes. We can distinguish, for example, between hard and soft varieties, between that which makes large demands on energy and resources and that characterized by high information content and advanced degree of social organization. We need to develop: sophisticated social technology—more emphasis on information exchange and less on transportation of goods and people; augmented social control of growth and management of distribution; and improved techniques for provision of public needs and less satisfaction of private demand by hard technology. Creation of a new reality image would change the operational definition of "technological progress" and consequent value judgments.

This new image of technology would be more compatible with the ecosystem reality image than would the present image as described above. It would show that in the future we must de-emphasize technologies highly consumptive of energy and resources or having severe environmental impact (Commoner, 1971). It might enable us, for example, to place increased emphasis on sophisticated backyard waste disposal in lieu of massive waste and sewage collection and treatment systems because of the dubious wisdom of using scarce water resources as a waste conveyance medium. Or, enable us to move toward energy conservation in the design of homes, using small-scale wind and solar energy sources rather than huge nuclear energy or coal-fired power grids so as to eliminate the waste heat problem. Or, to develop organic farming methods and desert greenhouses rather than vast monoculture and irrigation projects which use huge amounts of energy, fertilizers, and pesticides in order to avoid the chain of residual problems shown in figure 14.

Crucially important to the development of techno-social solutions is the development of a rational ecosystem approach to technology assessment. Technological policy assumes "that unwanted side effects or second-order consequences of technological development can be prevented or mitigated by 'technology assessment.'" If not well conceived and practiced, technology assessment will be in danger of becoming yet another narrow, disjointed incremental approach.

Technology assessment is in its infancy. Both the National Academy of Sciences and the National Academy of Engineering have recently issued reports on this subject (NAS, 1969; NAE, 1969). Methodologies for technology assessments are just being worked out (Coates, 1971; Jones, 1971). The National Environmental Protection Act has given additional impetus to this movement. Rational procedures (Leopold, 1971) for evaluating the impact on the environment of policy decisions which significantly involve the technology leverage variable have recently been proposed.

Unfortunately, one very fundamental issue in technology assessment is unresolved—the question of establishing the end purposes and priorities for assessments. Currently, the vogue is simply to look at a specific technology and assess it according to some methodology. This approach, however, does not provide much overall perspective and could degenerate into an extension or version of the market survey type of analysis for a new product. Clearly this approach is not comprehensive.

A rational ecosystem approach to technology assessment would be to place the technology to be assessed within the framework of the given societal need and evaluate the technologies within the range of technologies—present and projected—available to meet or satisfy human needs. It would be important in this approach to develop criteria by which to judge the desirability of one technology as opposed to another for meeting a societal need or function. A conceptual framework or scheme for selecting an appropriate technological response is shown in figure 16.

This approach to technology assessment would provide some comparative evaluation as to how well the possible techno-social solutions meet certain key criteria within an ecosystem framework. One possible output of such an assessment would be a clear indication that no present or foreseeable technology exists to meet certain demands imposed by projected population size and levels of consumption, at least not without incurring unacceptable risks. Such an indication, of course, would have very important policy implications for population and resource consumption planning.

Consequently, an ecosystem approach to technology assessment is essential in macrosystem policy research. Such research must propose a method for selecting from among alternative policies that one which is ecosystemically most compatible for reaching a desirable alternative future. A desirable future, however, cannot be determined until we measure the impacts of policies against the environmental constraints identified.

Selection of a Mix of Specific Policy Types

The comprehensive macrosystem approach to policy making demonstrates that a policy response to a particular so-

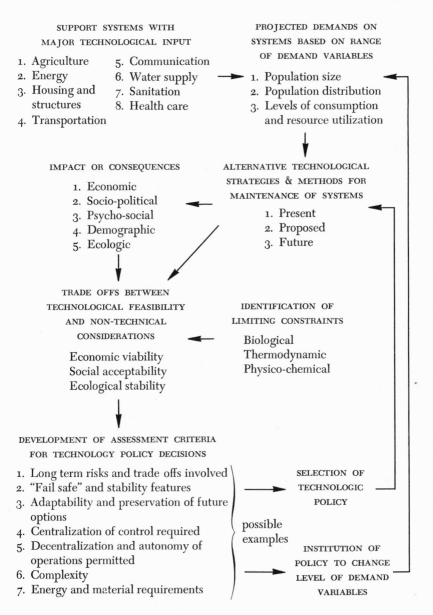

Fig. 16. A conceptual framework for selecting (and avoiding) technological responses to problems.

cio-environmental problem or need usually cannot be restricted to a single policy type. Analysis of the impact
space of a policy often will determine that multiple ecosystem linkages will be affected. In such an instance the
best policy response consists of a mix or combination of
policies assembled carefully from the possible specific policies in each of the four categories of policies classified
and discussed previously—population size, population
distribution, resource consumption, and technology.

One conceptual methodology for selecting and evaluating a mix of policy responses is as follows: The process
is initiated by a basic socio-environmental problem or
need. This perceived problem or need in turn generates a
spectrum of possible policy responses (or solutions to the
problem). Actual selection of a policy or mix of policies is
accomplished by some as yet undefined procedure. The
selection process is guided, however, by some combination of the judgmental descriptive elements related to
considerations of technical feasibility, economic viability,
ecological stability, and social acceptability. In addition,
the selection process is influenced by an understanding of
the likely impacts of various policy alternatives as identified by policy deliberations and determined with the use
of analytical models. The selected policy mix is then implemented and monitored through model simulation to
assess its primary (or intended) effectiveness and to ascertain its second-order consequences. During this monitoring stage, needed modifications in goals, strategy, and
tactics are introduced through a feedback process. Our
discussion in this section will illustrate the initial stages of
this general methodology and end with a more detailed
framework of this selection process. The use of analytical
models and model simulation will be discussed in chapter 5. A conceptual scheme for such a selection process is
shown in figure 17.

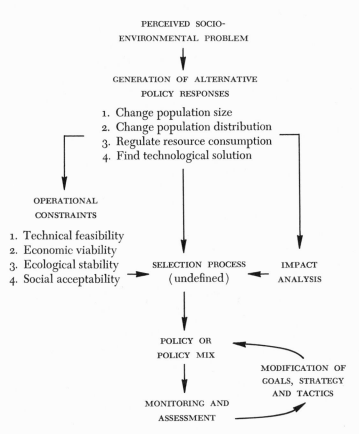

PERCEIVED SOCIO-
ENVIRONMENTAL PROBLEM

GENERATION OF ALTERNATIVE
POLICY RESPONSES

1. Change population size
2. Change population distribution
3. Regulate resource consumption
4. Find technological solution

OPERATIONAL
CONSTRAINTS

1. Technical feasibility
2. Economic viability
3. Ecological stability
4. Social acceptability

SELECTION PROCESS
(undefined)

IMPACT
ANALYSIS

POLICY OR
POLICY MIX

MODIFICATION OF
GOALS, STRATEGY
AND TACTICS

MONITORING AND
ASSESSMENT

Fig. 17. Conceptual scheme for policy mix selection and assessment.

A good way of illustrating the initial stages of selecting and evaluating a mix of policy responses is by example. We choose as our example the basic problem of FOOD PRODUCTION. At first glance this may seem a strange example to pick because hunger (but not necessarily malnutrition) is not yet widely regarded as a problem in the United States. Furthermore, our agriculture is widely hailed as one of our more spectacular successes. Food production and hunger, nevertheless, are major problems in much of the rest of the world. Even in the United States, recognition is dawning that the years of surplus and plenty may soon be over. Given present population projections, an agricultural crisis is likely to occur in traditional food production areas because of a shortage of either land or water. In addition, it could occur as a result of controls established to eliminate the deleterious environmental side effects of agricultural inputs (fertilizers, energy, and pesticides).

This problem, unlikely as it may seem at present, is explicitly recognized in the *Report of the Commission on Population Growth and the American Future* (1972). It is a major conclusion in the Institute of Ecology's *Report on Global Ecological Problems* (1972), and it is forcefully dramatized in *Limits to Growth* (Meadows et al., 1972). The latter (p. 50) shows that with exponential population growth, whether we double or quadruple agricultural production makes little difference in the time the supply of arable land will run out. Each doubling of production, for example, gains only about thirty years, or less than one population-doubling time, before the supply of arable land is exhausted.

The overall goal of our food production policy is to eliminate hunger with a minimum of human distress and environmental disruption.

Illustrative alternative policy responses (by type) to the problem of food production can be outlined by brief explanations of each:

1. *Limit population size*

Several alternatives and considerations are contained in this policy response. Population-size limitation will likely consist of stabilizing or limiting population growth

rates (and therefore the demand for food) in some specified fashion. Implicit in this policy response are various
means of limiting size, from manipulation of birth rates to
manipulation of death rates. Several alternatives available
to limit birth rates include:

a) *Voluntary birth control*
b) *Mandatory contraception*
c) *Economic incentives* (e.g., tax rebates for lack of
conception, lower taxes for smaller families, etc.)
d) *Social incentives* (e.g., privileges and leisure opportunities available only to small families)

The manipulation of the death rate could include policies
that establish socially acceptable criteria (i.e., the conditions under which serious considerations might be given)
for:

e) *Abortion*
f) *Euthanasia*
g) *Suicide*
h) *Capital offenses*

Many of these alternatives significantly depend upon
technological inputs, social values, and economic viabili-
ties; the most stringent policies would be considered
when the projected food-population balance becomes se-
verely upset.

2. *Change population distribution*

Policies on population distribution patterns are pertinent to food production in several ways. First, due to the
outward growth of urban areas and to their tendency to
locate on prime agricultural lands such as alluvial flood
plains, land-use conflicts are significant. Second, due to
the traditional patterns of development of cities (the establishment of an agricultural base, followed by trade and

industrial bases), the economic and geographic roles of agriculture change over time. Third, agricultural practices are constantly altered by changes in production, processing, communication, and distribution technologies, which occur more rapidly than do social institutional changes. Antiquated laws, inequitable resource evaluations, and social tensions result from the unequal rates of change.

In a general sense, each population distribution pattern affects food supply indirectly through its land-use requirements, the types of agriculture it fosters, and its influence on the flow of nutrients and wastes. Examples of population distribution policies include:

a) Graduated property tax rates

A policy of lower tax rates for agricultural lands adjacent to urban areas. Perhaps this could be accomplished by (1) lower tax rates on agricultural lands, or (2) a tax rebate for the owners of agricultural lands.

b) Compartmentalized zoning

c) Concentrated transportation and communication systems

A strategy to locate developmental stimuli (e.g., the selection of major transportation routes affects the location of future residential dwellings, support facilities, etc.).

d) Economic inducements to alter the rural-urban population migration trends

e) Transfer of urban organic wastes to strategically located farms

3. *Regulate or change food consumption patterns*

Attitudes underlying consumption practices are very diverse. They include the more obvious ones such as social pride, tradition, and level of economic development. Religious dietary taboos and advertising play an important role as well. Since consumption is based on a variety of factors, the policies on food consumption practices can take diverse forms:

a) *Food rationing* (e.g., to favor use of foods produced at lowest environmental costs)

b) *Production shift to foods more conservative of land and energy* (e.g., away from meat production)

c) *Packaging and advertising policy changes* (e.g., promotion of new foods using fish protein concentrates)

d) *Change of government price support policies* (e.g., alteration of government policies that create artificial supply and demand relationships)

e) *New values* (e.g., adoption of new values that support different consumption practices such as ecological living, organic foods, and durable "durable" goods)

4. *Increase food production by technology*

The United States has a traditional technological orientation toward solution of its problems and fulfillment of its needs. Because technological applications to our production systems have created a relatively high standard of living, we have developed a confidence in the ability of technology to satisfy all our needs. Even the current camping craze has a strong technological focus (recreational vehicles such as campers, trail bikes, ATV's, etc.).

In the production of food a rather large and varied range of technological alternatives exist. Various alternatives and their salient features are:

a) *Energy   intensive   monoculture*   (agro-industrial complexes)

These are high yield, open systems with little recycling of nutrients. They are characterized by low species and spatial diversity and, therefore, have low ecological stability. They can only be maintained by high inputs of fertilizer, pesticides, herbicides, and energy. They also rely heavily on an industrialized base (Odum, 1971).

b) *Labor   intensive   diversified   agriculture* (organic farming)

Typically a low yield, closed system with a minimum input of external, artificial energy. Soil fertility and humus content are maintained naturally through the recycling of plant residues and animal wastes.

c) *Aquaculture*

High yields are possible (figure 18 shows the relative biological productivity of aquatic and terrestrial systems). Artificial ponds utilizing detritus, sewage wastes, nutrient salts plus heated effluents have achieved high food production rates (as much as 300 tons/hectare/yr.). Other forms of aquaculture with higher energy and nutrient inputs can far exceed this tonnage.

d) *Shifting agriculture—tropics*

Generally regarded as a primitive, low-productivity type of agricultural technology. It is a highly advanced system, however, from the point of view of empirical ecology and most effective in the conservation of soil and nutrients in tropical regions, as long as rotation times are sufficient to permit restoration of soil nutrients and where particular slash and burn techniques do not destroy soil quality.

e) Biochemical synthesis of food

Involves conversion of cellulose into digestive sugars and proteins by processes similar to fermentation. Requires development of enzyme technologies. Would open up vast new food source from woody vegetation (see Odum, 1969; Institute of Ecology, 1972, p. 182), but could understandably alter ecosystem linkages if instituted widespread (e.g., the extensive processing of nonplantation, tropical forests).

f) Arid land agriculture

1. *Open field irrigation.* No climatic limitations on crops. Requires huge amounts of water in water deficit regions. Salinization of soil still a serious problem in irrigation projects.

2. *Desert greenhouses.* Plants are set directly in the sand and fed a water solution at their roots in climate-controlled, plastic, inflatable greenhouses. Desalinated ocean or brackish water can be used. Evaporation losses minimal in the greenhouse and no water is required for leaching, thus resulting in a considerable water saving over open-field irrigation ("Arid Land Agriculture," 1971).

Having outlined a range of alternative responses to the problem of food production, the next stage is to choose from among them. Although the policy selection process is an area for future research, we can use the food production example to show some of the principles needed to guide the selection process. In considering the policy menu, the technology, consumption, and population-distribution alternatives should be evaluated prior to those on population size. The ecological view of systems management requires that support capacities of the envi-

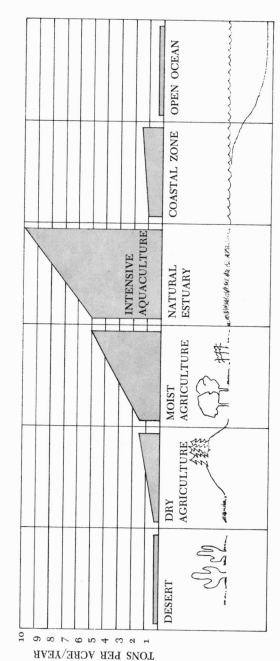

Fig. 18. Comparative production rates among terrestrial and aquatic systems (adapted from the *Institute of Ecology Report*, 1972, p. 250). Original source: J. M. Teal, and M. Teal, *Life and Death of a Salt Marsh* (Boston: Atlantic, Little, Brown and Co., 1969).

ronment be known before optimum population levels can be planned. The same situation can be put into focus with a discussion of needs. As mentioned previously, the methodology for the selection of a policy mix is initiated by a perception of a need, with this perception taking into account the fact that needs and policy responses to them can have a positive feedback effect unless the needs themselves are controlled. For example, increasing the size of a population results in increasing food needs, which stimulate larger food production systems, which in turn encourages population growth, and so forth. The positive feedback trend continues until the population can no longer tolerate nonfood environmental stresses (e.g., space), or the life support abilities of the ecosystem have been reduced or surpassed. When these limits are reached, the population size could collapse because of a sudden increase in deaths. Therefore, it would be desirable to "break the positive feedback loop" by determining how large a population the ecosystem can support and stabilizing the population size accordingly.

In contrast to this approach, the conventional policy response to food production problems has been to seek a technological solution, that is, to increase food production with energy intensive, high yield monoculture (alternative 4a, p. 124). Large irrigation projects are crucial to this approach. The deficiencies and limitations in the approach have been discussed. In addition to these, the "law of diminishing returns" appears to militate against continued growth of this type of agriculture. The nature of this law of diminishing returns is illustrated in figure 19, which clearly shows the nonlinear relationship between agricultural output per unit area (yield) and input (fertilizers).

At some point the maintenance costs in an inten-

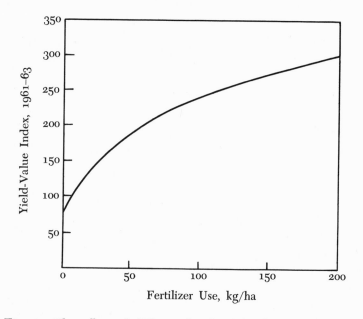

Fig. 19. The effect of different levels of fertilizer use on the yield-value index, 1961–63 (adapted from the *Institute of Ecology Report*, 1972, p. 16). Original source: *The World Food Problem*, III, Panel on the World Food Supply (Washington, D.C.: Government Printing Office, 1967).

sively managed system exceed the value derived. Maintenance costs in a high-yield agriculture go into fertilizer, pesticides, and energy. As these expenditures increase, there is less and less rate of increase in yield, as shown in figure 19. In the future, additional maintenance costs could be incurred or assessed for pollution damage resulting from agricultural practices. For example, there could be nitrate contamination of surface and ground water, as shown in figure 20. Additional maintenance costs would

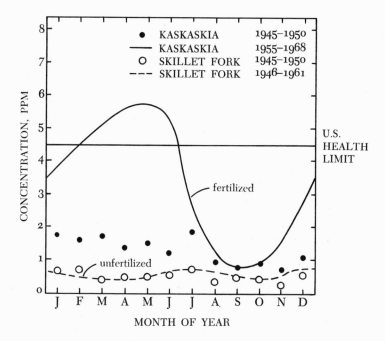

Fig. 20. Nitrate levels in river waters in fertilized (Kaskaskia) and unfertilized (Skillet Fork) basins (adapted from the *Institute of Ecology Report,* 1972, p. 66). Original source: T. E. Larson and B. D. Larson, "Quality of Surface Water in Illinois," *Interim Report on the Presence of Nitrate in Illinois Surface Waters* (Urbana: Illinois State Water Survey, 1968).

bring into consideration judgmental-value premises and ecosystem considerations.

The difference between the gross yield value and the maintenance costs for a given technological food production policy defines a net yield curve which will contain an optimum. These relationships are schematically illustrated in figure 21. This optimum establishes the maxi-

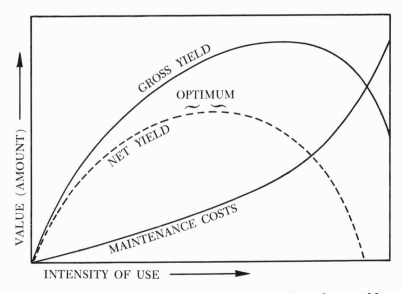

Fig. 21. Trends in gross yield, maintenance costs and net yield with increasing intensity of use (adapted from the *Institute of Ecology Report*, p. 133).

mum yield one can expect from that particular technological policy, assuming proper assessment of maintenance costs. Even if a particular policy should provide satisfactory yields, the tendency toward the acceptance of the minimum "satisficing policy" (March and Simon, 1958) is to be avoided since (1) unevaluated alternatives to the "satisficing" one may prove superior; (2) a mix of policies may have synergic interactions that produce higher yields under more desirable circumstances; and (3) a mixture of policies is more conducive to ecosystem stability.

The reason for the conventional policy response of seeking just a technological solution is that the decision maker often remains bewildered by the vast array of policy choices presented when alternative policies are generated, even if he does desire to consider them in a systematic manner. One useful method for the consideration of policy mixes is a technique using what we have named the "dra-graph" (fig. 22). The dra-graph is basically qualitative in nature; it is a tool for subjective analysis. It provides a methodology for helping policy researchers narrow a large number of possible policy mixes to a manageable number for serious consideration.

The dra-graph has some characteristics similar to a signed "digraph" (Harary, Norman, and Cartwright, 1965). Essentially an interaction web with pair-wise links, the dra-graph indicates by the use of positive (+) or negative (−) signs whether the policy interactions in a group of policies reinforce each other or are counteractive. The pattern of signs in the interaction web indicates the policy mix or set of compatible alternative policies worthy of further consideration.

With the dra-graph technique the policy researcher first lists all available possibilities under their respective categories (e.g., population distribution, resource consumption, etc.), as illustrated in the mixture of food production policies in figure 22. The population distribution, resource consumption, and technology policies initially are considered apart from population size policies. This is in accordance with the ecosystem principle mentioned earlier in this section. Once the policies have been organized into categorical lists, each policy in one category is evaluated with each policy in the other categories, two at a time.

This evaluation stage constitutes the core of the technique. In the food production example, we based our evaluations on considerations of ecosystem interactions, one of the groups of judgmental descriptive elements used in the policy classification scheme outlined pre-

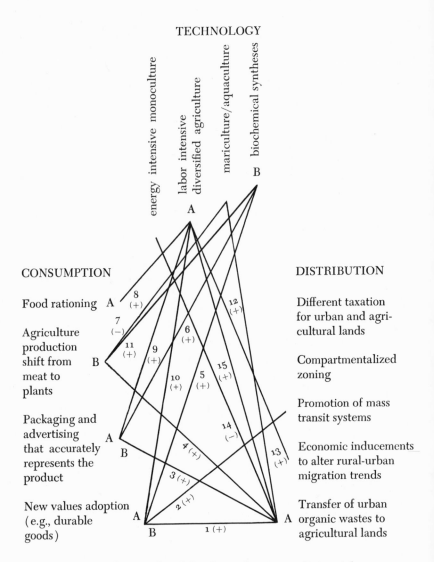

Fig. 22. A dra-graph of food production policies (the eco-systemic rationale for the signed links is explained on p. 131). A and B represent ecosystemically compatible (+) sets of policies. Numbers indicate interaction links and are explained on page 133–34.

Linkage
Numbers   *Explanation of Figure 22*

1,3.   If the people are to accept the idea of using human wastes for agricultural purposes, an alteration of their attitudes is necessary. For many decades health departments have warned citizens of the dangers of recycling human feces. The fear of contamination of food stocks will have to be overcome by skillful advertising.

2.   For similar reasons, advertising and the adoption of new values are necessary to alter ingrained traditions and attitudes toward automobiles, etc.

5,6.   Similarly, alterations of attitudes are needed concerning food production by biochemical synthesis.

4.   Since organic wastes are to be used for agricultural production, this policy is quite compatible with a policy advocating a greater proportion of plant matter in food production.

7.   Maricultural and aquacultural processes usually involve the growth of animals like shrimp or catfish. This production trend is contrary to an agricultural production shift from meat to plants.

8.   At the present time, rural areas are too scarce of workers to raise enough food by organic farming methods. The scarcity of food products would cause food rationing.

9,10.   Since organic produce is likely to be blemished, at least initially until natural systems of pest control can be established, new values and advertising efforts are necessary for general adoption of labor intensive diversified agriculture by the public.

11.   Since biochemical synthesis involves the degradation of plant materials, and plants constitute the single cell protein (SCP) organisms, biochemical synthesis indeed is compatible with the agricultural production shift from animals to plants.

12.   Slowing down the migration of rural laborers to urban areas would be a boon for labor intensive diversified agriculture. The labor supply would be where it was needed.

13.   The organic wastes would supply nutrients for the growth of plants, forming the basis of the mariculture food chains.

14.   Since urban wastes would supply the farms with waste nutrients, the traditional energetic fertilizer applications would not be needed. Thus, the policies are not compatible.

15.   Organic farming and waste reuse both involve recycling perspectives; thus, they are compatible.

viously (fig. 10). Additional dra-graphs for the other categories of judgmental elements (value premises and operational considerations), as shown in figure 10, can be constructed. For these, the dra-graph technique would be particularly useful in evaluating policy mixes because at the present time few models are suitable for analysis.

Since the bases for sign evaluations can be determined by economic costs, expected political feasibilities, environmental factors such as air pollution levels, or any combination of such criteria, the dra-graph approach is very flexible. The major evaluation requirement is for the policy researcher to have unambiguous evaluation criteria that he explicitly understands. If an ecosystem rationale indicates that any two policies being evaluated are strongly compatible, the interaction between them is given a positive sign; if it indicates a strongly negative interaction, a negative sign is given. For clarity of the dra-graph, we have not shown the neutral or weak interactions in our food production example. A more sophisticated development of the technique would indicate the relative magnitude of the signs (e.g., +0.7). This would be significant if synergic opportunities were to be considered.

Once the policy interactions have been evaluated, the policy researcher traces the patterns of positive interactions among the different categories to ascertain the sets of policy mixes based upon his evaluation criteria. In the food production example, it can be seen that the ecosystemically compatible sets (A and B) include the following policies:

	Consumption	*Technology*	*Distribution*
Set A	Packaging and advertising that accurately represents the product	Labor intensive diversified agriculture	Transfer of urban wastes to agricultural lands
	Adoption of new values		
	Food rationing		
Set B	Agricultural production shift from meat to plants	Biochemical syntheses	
	Packaging and advertising that accurately represents the product		
	Adoption of new values		

The next stage in our methodology is to consider more precisely the ecosystemic impact of the different policy mixes. The above mixes of three categories of policies must also be combined with compatible alternative policies in the population size category. In performing this final exercise many tradeoffs among the policy mixes need to be considered. Particularly helpful is the use of analytical models to predict ecosystem impacts of policy mixes. In addition, we need to establish criteria making broad tradeoffs between policy options. This ultimately amounts to a choice among alternative futures. Final consideration, then, of a specific policy mix cannot be made until the evaluation is brought up to the level of an overview for action.

Chapter V

Macrosystems Synthesis for Decision Making

The preceding discussion has made clear the necessity of approaching policy problems by means of a process that recognizes three important factors:

1. The separate but commingled pervasiveness of reality, value, and instrumental judgments in social decision making.

2. Classification of policies and impacts according to ecosystem and human value categories.

3. A technological-social calculus that can deal with the transformation of policies into impacts and value implications.

To amalgamate these factors into the policy-making process, we suggest the use of analytical models.

Analytical Models as Tools for Policy Making
Analytical or mathematical models have been successfully used in industrial, commercial, and military decision making as well as in the study of population biology and environmental dynamics. In these traditional uses they are identified with the rational and objective approach. Their use in social policy making, however, has been controversial (Chen, 1972). By taking into account the pervasiveness of judgments in modeling, the controversy may be understood and perhaps resolved.

137

Modeling methodology traditionally involves three steps. The first step is to develop "process physics." This is the description of known or hypothesized relations among the variables under consideration. The second step is to formalize and state the measures of performance (or measures of effectiveness) that serve as criteria for evaluating the system being modeled. The third step is to identify and explore the effects of the control variables— the factors, constraints, or parameters available to be adjusted, within limits, by the policy maker.

These three steps of the modeling procedure conveniently parallel the three judgmental categories outlined previously. Reality judgment identifies the important variables (in terms of impact or policy possibilities) to include in the model, as well as prescribes the kinds of process physics that get developed. Value judgment determines the type, dimensions, scales, and limits for the measures of performance. Instrumental judgment directly provides identification, description, and statement of options for the control variables. Thus, the use of an analytical model recognizes the first necessary important factor in developing an approach to policy making.

The second factor, the classification of policies and impacts according to ecosystem and human value categories, is entirely compatible with and complementary to the use of analytical models. For example, the leverage variables and their corresponding lower-level variables will appear in an analytical model based on the ecosystem image. The analysis of value implications will complement the mathematical experimentation on the analytical model. The third factor actually requires the use of analytical models. The development of the transformations to describe the passage from the policy space to the impact space of figure 2 (p. 18) must be accomplished by the use of analytical models. Consideration of the tens of performance measures, the hundreds of relationships, and the thousands of variables involved in even the simplest of social systems requires analytical techniques—if only to decide which elements to ignore.

Primitive mental models exist now and are used to develop these transformations. These imprecise "mental images" of process and structure, cause and event, and data and inference indeed are models. They are constructs of the real world that provide images with which to test hypotheses or perform "mind experiments." They are subject to vagaries of time and hidden inconsistencies, however, and suffer from unknown degrees of subjectivity. This process of internalization influences not only the transformations between policies and impacts, but the instances in which policies will be made. Many "instantaneous zero population growth" policies apparently have their origins in such mental models of process.

Perhaps the most important contribution of formal modeling is the requirement that assumptions made about policy alternatives, impacts, and their relations be explicit. The model focuses criticism upon these assumptions and forces critics to be equally explicit in their attacks. To do this, the language of a good model necessarily must be clear. Alternatives must be spelled out; elements left out must be obviously so. In addition, measures of performance force operational definitions on otherwise loose words such as "good," "favorable," and "socially destructive." This is not to say that the model omits subjective considerations; instead, it makes them explicit. Subjectivity may be encoded by probability assignments and utility functions (or preference orderings). In fact, the choice of which model structure to use is a fundamentally subjective one.

Mathematical models give us the ability to handle the large amounts of data and the complex combinations of factors necessary to clearly link policies to impacts. This is particularly the case when the national ramifications of a specific environmental policy are considered. Even the best of informal structures cannot allow for the vast number of dependencies among the hominisphere, biosphere, atmosphere, lithosphere, and hydrosphere, each dependency in turn involving many sets of numbers and relationships (Glass and Watt, 1971).

A mathematical model, over time and use, acquires a degree of veracity—a relationship to the "real world" that is believable. Since the output variables of analytical models are operationally defined, it is a straightforward procedure to test the models against causal events in the system being modeled. Thus, a model that purports to describe the interaction between population growth and environmental effects in the less-developed countries can be checked (or "calibrated") by comparing its output with that of selected countries. Once developed, a model furthermore allows for adaption and change as our substantive knowledge changes. This ability to take specific advantage of feedback and criticism is of particular value in the political environment of growth policy.

Contribution to the community's "shared image" of reality is an extremely important advantage of modeling. Laying clear a specific set of transformations between the policy space and the impact space may be all that experienced executives or policy makers need in order to agree upon important points, or at least to agree as to where they disagree. Thus, inclusion of the policy maker in the development of the model initially adds to its veracity and hence use of the results. Particularly in the area of environmental research, the use of models to communicate would allow large numbers of people to establish areas of mutual agreement and point the way to research needs in controversial areas. In addition, in a rational era a mathematical model properly used and interpreted could "sell" policy decisions to constituencies. Decision making not buttressed with models would become suspect.

Of particular importance for policy research is that analytical models also are learning tools (Dunn, 1971). For example, the construction of quantitative social hypotheses relating population policies to environmental effects may be valuable just for the insights gained into the fundamental social phenomena being studied. A model especially will reveal lacks of knowledge. In fact, if knowledge about the relationships between policies and ecosystem impacts is insufficient to build models, then there is little rational justification for making decisions involving the particular systems.

In order to use analytical models for policy making, however, the policy researcher has to be aware of certain reservations about the use of models, particularly in the analysis of growth policy. For instance, the modeling effort, by diverting attention and intellectual resources, may detract from other efforts at understanding. These other efforts may be verbal descriptions or intuitive interpretations of observations and data which in the long run could have a greater impact on the policy maker, and thus a more constructive potential.

In addition, the researcher who develops analytical models of large systems often starts from one of two comfortable initial points—a "stripped down" (admittedly simple) representation of the complex system, or a special technique or tool with which he is familiar and in which he is unwittingly encapsulated (e.g., differential equations). Either approach can stifle further development. The researcher could insist on "building on" the pilot model, or on using a variation of "the technique." This kind of intellectual incrementalism in model building is difficult to prevent; it is even more difficult to correct once considerable effort has been expended.

When developing his model the policy researcher should not be isolated from those responsible for policy decisions, that is, from those who will use it. The modeler can easily "assume," for example, a social welfare function, $f(P,F,E)$, relating social good to population, food, and energy. A policy maker, lacking a better way of expressing his own image of the relation, conceivably could even use such an assumption. Whether he actually would accept the output of the model, however, is something else again, particularly if his job or public image is at stake.

The researcher must use particular care in his model when dealing with uncertainty. He often lacks the information necessary to completely specify the model. Detailed understanding of the functional relationships between policies and impacts of social, population, and environmental processes is woefully unavailable. Whether particular relationships are linear or nonlinear, independent or dependent, time-lagged or decayed, causal or coincidental, is not really known.

Even when the relationships are known, the problem remains of determining the numerical values of the parameters involved. Some (such as the gross birth rate for California twenty years from now) are basically random variables, and thus "knowable" only in terms of a probabilistic description. Others (the assignable cost per kilowatt hour of electricity generated by a tower-cooled nuclear plant) might be determined precisely with enough effort and experimentation. The problems are to design efficient experiments for obtaining precise values for these parameters and to develop practical procedures for eliciting probability descriptions.

There is also a fundamental uncertainty in describing reasonable output variables. Even if the modeler takes into account the fact that these are in themselves to some degree unknown, he must decide what they should be in the first place. The identification of performance measures is not a trivial exercise. In fact, it is dependent on individual and group value judgments. For this reason it is perhaps the most critical but underemphasized part of model building. The use of Gross National Product as an output proxy for a society's "success" or "quality of life" must be examined as critically as the use of "crop yield" as a criterion of agricultural success.

One fundamental uncertainty overrides all others—will the socioenvironmental system we are trying to model remain reasonably stable during the time frame of the model representation? Whether the causes of instability are physical, biological, or social is irrelevant to the basic problem of obtaining information concerning this possible system variation with time.

The use of an analytical model becomes extremely valuable for policy makers who must deal with such uncertainties in socioenvironmental systems. A model serves to identify critical variables and relationships and reveals the implications of having imperfect information about the system. It may predicate uncertain factors, and then can be used to analyze various assumptions made about the uncertain elements. For example, it may be unclear as to what the electricity consumption rate in New York City would be as the result of implementing a specific effluent charge on power companies. A model could be exercised with a range of consumption rates, and the output examined to see if the model is significantly affected. If it is not, precise knowledge of the rate is irrelevant; if it is, then further research must be devoted to determining the price elasticity of electric power. Certain parameter values, however, assumed to be intrinsically "unknowable" by definition, become random variables with probability descriptions that are either experimentally or subjectively derived. The outputs thus become random variables, with the model supplying their probability descriptions.

Models also serve to develop structures for resolving controversies. Different decision makers or decision-making groups have different models as a result of different reality judgments. Analysis and use of the different models would lead to mutual understanding of views, interests, and conclusions (in terms of policy recommendations). This procedure also could suggest alternative policies in some sense superior to existing alternatives in all models. In fact, this technique is useful for both the communication and the pedagogical tasks required for policy making. If a participant raises the argument that "the system is so complicated that it can't possibly be analytically described," the modeler can hypothetically pose "critical" input and output parameters and ask the objector, as a start, to establish a simple relation between them. The modeling activity would proceed as the complexities of the relation are elaborated.

Analytical models force the policy researcher to attempt to determine meaningful performance measures— of assigning values to elements in the impact space. Specific measures are now being identified for the population-environment impact space: growth rates, DDT levels, GNP. Such simple measures, of questionable utility by themselves, can be extremely useful as a means of eliciting from policy makers alternative measures they would prefer. In addition, analytical models force the policy researcher to attempt to measure the attainment of population or environmental policy goals. Even if the appropriate variables are clearly identified, the long time-constants of the system and the natural "noise" inherent in it add to the formidable problems associated with determining, storing, and manipulating the values of social variables. Essential to successful modeling here is a program of accurate, unbiased record-keeping, as well as storage and retrieval capabilities. On a global scale such efforts are clearly the responsibility of multinational organizations. For building and evaluating models on a local or tactical level, however, such efforts are equally important (Tietze, Chow and Mauldin in Berelson, 1966).

Policy makers often seek simplicity because simple analysis is easy to explain, and the public responds to simple answers and explanations. This may account, for example, for proposals of extremely stringent (perhaps unenforceable) antipollution legislation. Models unfortunately can render complex situations simple, and consequently be used as propaganda tools. It is almost certain that any oversimplified "solutions" will exacerbate rather than assuage the problems and the debates.

Thus, the development of complex analytical models for policy research into the problems associated with population and the environment may be necessary before solutions can be derived. One way to accomplish this, and simultaneously to involve the policy maker effectively and account for factors that perhaps cannot be modeled, is to use the Gaming Simulation technique. The process of developing policy points (that make up the policy space) and deciding which points will produce favorable impacts may be described as: joint dynamic decision making under uncertainty. Because of the requirements for group decisions (involving social and psychological interactions from the lowest to highest degree) in an ever-changing environment (about which little is understood or certain), many people have argued that a truly useful model must involve people and the actual uncertainties and time progression contained, in a physically and psychologically "realistic" setting. Short of allowing policy makers to "play" with the real world, an exact "model" of this sort cannot exist. Thus an often useful approximation is the gaming simulation. This technique has had success in such diverse areas as industrial management, urban and regional planning, fish and wildlife management, water resource usage, and military operations (see Naylor, 1969, for a list of references).

A gaming simulation could take into account many complexities in the relationships between population and environmental factors. More important, it would recognize the political, social, economic, and organizational constraints on actions, and that policy decisions relate to effects far in the future. In addition, a gaming simulation might recognize modifications of individual decisions by the possibly independent decision making of planners in education, agriculture, defense, or health who do not necessarily consider the demographic or environmental effects in their decisions or goal statements.

A simulation allows individuals to play roles in the decision process. They may be given an "objective function" by which their performance is measured. Each role-playing decision maker then, subject to constraints (some of which may be unknown or unclear), sets control variables (in effect, creates strategies and tactics) to achieve his goals. The simulation, by means of some predetermined structure (because of the complexity involved, many gaming simulations make use of computers to keep track of what is happening), provides the transformation of control variable settings (i.e., policies) along with uncontrollable variables representing natural phenomena into impacts. These impacts in turn are fed back (possibly through filters or delays) to the decision makers, and the process continues.

Such gaming techniques to study population issues (Packer and Moreland, 1969) and environmental issues (Feldt, 1972) could be useful if the following points are kept in mind:

1. It is a useful training technique; real policy makers can play their own roles, but try various strategies in the simulation.

2. It is a sensitizing technique; the roles of, for example, consumer and producer or population planner and economic planner may be reversed to clarify each other's images.

3. It is valuable for determining the psychological and social "critical variables," analogous to the way mathematical models can pinpoint critical physical, economic, and demographic variables.

4. It should not, however, be used as a normative (prescriptive) tool; the structure (a mathematical model, if for no other reason than the fact that a computer is used) is often subservient to the portions involving human interactions in the development of the simulation. To paraphrase Lucas (1959): gaming is never likely to produce a calculus of policy, but it may well provide a device by which we sharpen our logical teeth and develop our ecological perceptions.

Existing Models

Some of these techniques already have been used in policy research and policy making. Those familiar with research into the population and environment area know that an important initial use of the analytical approach is in the models of *World Dynamics* (Forrester, 1971) and the *Limits to Growth* (Meadows et al., 1972). *Limits to Growth*, phase one of the Club of Rome's Project on the Predicament of Mankind, makes a bold attempt to model global population-environmental interactions.

This approach has many of the attributes we specified above. The model made explicit assumptions regarding structure and parameter values. Truly constructive criticism (for example, Ridker, 1972), took exception to specific assumptions. Where intuition was inserted into the model (and it certainly was in many places), it was done explicitly. Persons with different images of structures or parameter values could present their interpretations of the underlying process. The model enables critical elements to be identified as well as elements to which the system appears to be insensitive (this is not to say that the world itself will be insensitive to these variables, but simply that the model is).

In addition, the model was able, by its conclusions, to challenge traditional approaches to the implications of growth. It forced a debate (which will apparently continue for many years) concerning the fundamental relationships between such global parameters as population level, pollution, and amount of natural resources available. In this particular case, the output was quite understandable and in a form that both the layman and policy maker could understand. Consequently, the model has forced a great many people in many arenas to reassess some of their fundamental beliefs and images. The policy-making environment has been noticeably affected.

We will not repeat the specific criticisms leveled at *The Limits to Growth* model (e.g., Gillette, 1972; Shubik, 1971; Passell, Roberts, and Ross, 1972). Instead, we identify six categories of criticism that suggest steps that might be taken to use this work to develop better models of the policy-to-impact transformation process:

1. The high level of aggregation of the model—the use of only five basic variables—is such that it is very hard to determine whether the linking structure is realistic.

2. The changes in variable levels depend only upon previous levels of these variables, not on the change rates of these levels. Thus, the birth rate depends upon the number of people at the previous time period, not on how rapidly the number of people has been increasing over the past few time periods.

3. There is no open reference to the fact that many of the variables involved are random variables. The probabilistic elements in the models are submerged in total aggregated variables. Thus, there is a tacit use of expected values, which is not appropriate for a model presuming to describe future (and thus basically unknowable) events.

4. There is no allowance for adaptation within the model. The model structure remains basically the same no matter what society learns. Attempts have been made by the Club of Rome and others to relax this assumption; nonetheless, it exists in the fundamental model.

5. There is a lack of differentiation of the behavior of the developed portion as compared to that of the less-developed portion of the world. (This is, in fact, a specific variant of category 1 and it is important enough to highlight here.) The fact that population in the developed portion of the world, which uses resources at a rapid rate, might in fact strongly affect the less-developed portion is a critical matter. Similarly, the fact that high growth rates are more prevalent in the less-developed portion of the

world should have an effect on the usage of resources in those areas as well as on the distribution of available resources.

This criticism, however, does not detract from the importance of the approach—the use of analytical models to explore global relationships between population and the environment.

Another shortcoming of the *The Limits to Growth* model emerges when it is contrasted to more familiar and traditional economic-demographic models:

6. The model has no economically based pricing or market structure; the demands for goods and services are essentially exogenous. Thus, the model has little equilibrium-seeking behavior.

Economic-demographic models, in contrast, can be extended to take into account short-term environmental repercussions (Leontief, 1970), but often slight long-term ecosystem concerns. Much of the research on modeling the interactions between economic and demographic variables has been concerned with such specific problems as the effects of income levels on fertility (Holmberg, 1970) or the relation between age structure and capital formation (Enke, 1971). The first of the more comprehensive models was the one used to describe the economic effects of different patterns of population growth in India (Coale and Hoover, 1958). Since then, a number of models have tested propositions of greater complexity: Shultz (1969) relates population growth to the economy of Puerto Rico; Barlow (1969) treats the level of fertility in underdeveloped countries as an endogenous variable; Davies (1972) simulates the effects of demographic factors on the Canadian economy.

Most of these models, however, lack direct comments

on the environmental, hence ecosystem, consequences of the various economic-demographic systems described. Others that do account for environmental variables lack clear linkages to population and/or economic interactions. For example, the monumental study underway of California's land, energy, and pollution interactions (Glass and Watt, 1971) contains no allowance for changes in the distribution of population or for possible concurrent policy-instituted changes in consumption patterns. Similarly, the Lake Tahoe regional simulation (Young, Arnold and Brewer, 1972) accounts for many social variables but no specifically ecosystemic ones.

The advantage of most of these models developed to analyze aspects of the economic-demographic-environmental system is that they include known process physics —fundamental physical principles (energy flows, evaporative processes), economic empirical relations (agricultural production functions, supply-demand curves) or elaborate multivariate statistical analyses (regressions relating birth rates to family incomes). They also include a large number of variables and relations, which lends credibility to their outputs.

Analytical models that expressly include economic behavior hold promise. For use in policy making, however, these models must be believable and persuasive as well as precise and encompassing. Many derive their coefficients from statistical data which depend heavily on the way society behaves and organizes itself (e.g., the specific technology with which society produces goods and services to meet demands, and the demands for goods and services as a function of income, age, etc.). To the extent that these coefficients will not change drastically within a relatively short time frame (1½ to 3 years), the models may have considerable predictive power. For the relatively long time frames (10 to 30 years) of ecosystem concerns, such economic models are not likely to be useful.

One way to stretch the time frames is to project the changes of coefficients through some sort of forecasting technique predicated on various policy assumptions. This implies the construction of cybernetic models, the use of subjective expert opinion, and a departure from the empirical base of econometric models. Although it is not clear how far the time frames should be extended to make the models useful to policy makers for population and environmental systems, with time frames extended far enough, macro-socio-economic models could have impacts at least as great as *The Limits to Growth* model.

Alternative Futures as a Macro-planning Approach

Another method of approaching policy research in the macroproblem area is to investigate alternative futures. Such an approach is not completely independent of the modeling approach, especially with models having long time frames, but it warrants separate consideration. Alternative futures planning does not require the precision that modeling does and has the potential to expand the images and judgmental capacities of the researcher. Such planning forces the researcher to think about basic issues and not to lose sight of the overview for action.

Growth policy is so encompassing and long-range in its impact that the choice of any mix of specific policies is tantamount to choosing our future. In this kind of macro-planning the concept of alternative futures serves to keep the significance of the policy mix from being submerged by considerations of specific policy types.

The description of alternative futures often takes the

form of a "scenario" (which probably derives from traditional concepts of possible futures as utopias and fictions). A scenario description is developed by means of systematic procedure of three steps:

1. Descriptive scenario generation—what the world is like today and what its future will be if current trends continue (especially the prevailing values, beliefs, and basic assumptions of the society).

2. Normative scenario generation—what the world would be like if what is desired according to the various value systems should come true (especially those basically different from the prevailing one).

3. Policy alteration—what policy changes would be necessary to alter current trends to achieve transition toward what is desired.

The procedure assumes that man's volition and knowledge give him the capability to influence his own future. It projects a time frame in the range of 10 to 50 years because society is difficult to alter significantly within a shorter frame due to inertia, and is difficult to map toward a more remote future due to too many unknowns (Platt, 1971). Within this time frame the procedure generates alternative futures, and then maps backward from each desirable future to determine what present-day policy alterations would be necessary. As explained in chapter 2 with reference to figure 2, this inverse transformation procedure is a useful way to introduce unconventional thinking. The discussion on policy mix also illustrates a procedure that starts with an alternative future and works back to suggest policy alterations. In that example, we began with a future society based on an ecosystem image. Then we determined policies on population distribution, resource consumption, and technology which would be consistent with that reality image. The alternative population policies could then be evaluated along with their value implications and the likely ecosystem consequences if those policies were not implemented.

This procedure has dynamic characteristics because the policy maker's image of reality changes over time and the world itself changes due to exogenous factors or in reaction to the macroplan (often counter to macroplan intentions). The three steps are repeated as society changes and the ecosystem reacts (resulting in different descriptive scenarios), as the policy maker's values shift (resulting in different normative scenarios), and as the policy maker learns from program evaluation and social and technological experimentation (resulting in different perceptions of the causal relationships between policy actions and social and environmental variables).

These three steps in the macroplanning procedure based on the concept of alternative futures correspond to the three kinds of judgment and contain all the implications of subjectivity. The descriptive scenario generation corresponds to reality judgment (*what is*). The choice and interpretation of social indicators which describe social trends are subjective, as well as the diagnosis of undesirable symptoms in a particular descriptive scenario. The second step, normative scenario generation, corresponds to value judgment (*what should be*), which by definition is subjective. The third step, policy alteration, corresponds to instrumental judgment (*what to do*). As discussed earlier, identification of the causal relationships between social policies and their consequences usually involves subjective judgment. Divergent opinions on practical policy options can be traced to differences in basic assumptions about human nature (Theobald, 1968). The value implications of specific policies are subjective. In sum, the ideology of means is as formidable as the ideology of ends (Rein, 1971).

Although almost every step in macroplanning involves subjective judgment, whether one uses modeling or alternative futures as the central approach, subjectivity does not undermine the usefulness of the procedure. Once subjectivity is recognized, there are ways of accounting for it and of using it. One way is for the policy researcher to take a deliberately critical stance (Etzioni, 1971) with respect to the subjective judgment implied by the established policy. Another way is for the policy researcher to do the macroplanning from a number of subjective viewpoints and to identify the policy alternatives that are "Pareto optimum"; ° that is, optimum in the sense that no social segment can gain relative to its own value system without hurting other social segments relative to their value systems. Still another way is for the policy researcher to play the role of a change agent, who would skillfully help the policy maker and policy-influencing groups examine and eventually modify their basic values and images.

As with modeling, the writing of alternative futures has been systematized and applied extensively to military planning (Kahn, 1964), but in the growth policy area further work is needed. A number of articles and books have suggested various attributes of growth patterns for the United States that could be fundamentally different from the growth pattern that will most likely result from the continuation of current policy trends. However, these

° A "Pareto-optimal" allocation of resources is one such that no other allocation can simultaneously improve the conditions (i.e., increase the utility) for everyone involved. Thus, in a Pareto-optimal policy, if someone is made better off, someone else must be made worse off (Pareto, 1927).

writings have not carefully analyzed the mutual compatibility and self-consistency of the suggested attributes. We need to identify possible new paradigms for future growth, and to describe explicitly the corresponding alternative futures with sufficient detail and credibility so that all major social groups can take these alternative futures seriously, and appreciate what these alternative futures mean to them. We also need to develop a systematic procedure for comparing and selecting alternative futures and the corresponding alternative policy combinations regardless of the subjective criteria used.

Criteria for Selection Among Policy Alternatives

Selection of a policy requires an examination of potential impacts and some procedure for deciding their relative desirabilities. At this point three elements of the fundamental problem of choice become intertwined, often to the disadvantage of policy research:

1. Accounting for personalistic or subjective desires needed to handle ethical and psychological as well as economic problems.

2. Understanding of group decision processes—formal and informal—involved when policy must be made in conjunction with others and regarding impacts on yet others.

3. Appreciation for the way decisions are (or should be) made in the face of uncertainties—particularly about events over which the policy maker feels he has no control.

Certain logical procedures can take these elements into account, without which some means of achieving social consensus may be counterproductive. For example, freedom fragmented and distributed among small, individual decisions may work against the freedom of society as a whole, which in turn limits the options open to all the individuals in the society. The tradeoffs in such cases must be studied systematically. Even incrementalists agree that the "muffled rationality which is the outcome of political bargaining . . . can take place only when all groups . . . have access to the political process" (Rein, 1971, p. 306).

In order to make a choice, that is, a policy decision, there of course must be a set of alternatives. How to make these explicit was the subject of previous sections. Now we must concern ourselves with the reasons for particular choices among alternatives. When treating a single-person, nonprobabilistic problem, a decision involves an ordering of preferences among the outcomes associated with policies, and choosing that which is, subjectively, "best." This procedure, of course, is not necessarily conscious or admitted, and is more tautological. It is important to note, however, that this description holds even for moral issues. Boulding states that ethics may be regarded as a set of ordered preferences (Callahan, 1972).

Often, when more than one major element is involved in categorizing impacts, it is convenient to express one's preferences as isopotential lines on a multidimensional figure. (For purely economic problems it is often convenient to collapse all of these dimensions into one—profit, for example, in a commercial context.) The choice, then, is to find a policy that has, within given constraints, the highest preference.

For example, consider the yield-fertilizer problem discussed in "Selection of a Mix of Policies." Although it may be put into purely economic terms, it is also possible to develop a "utility" (preference) function for an individual as shown in figure 23. Each curve is a locus of points of indifference, and therefore constant utility (equal preference). This individual is relatively insensitive to ecological damage if the crop yield is low (his preferences are much like those of planners in a less-developed country); if the yield is fairly high, a large increase in yield is required to compensate for the additional ecological damage.

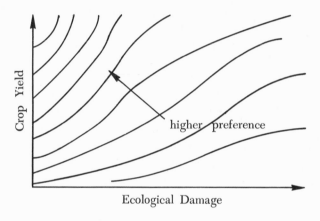

Fig. 23. Curves of equal utility for the yield-fertilizer example.

The theory behind establishing such preference functions for actual situations is far enough advanced (see, for example, Keeney, 1972) so as to dispute Rein (1971, pp. 304–5) when he writes, "[rational analysis] places its faith on the assumption that information facilitates 'good' decisions, but it offers no criteria for judging what is a good decision except the circular argument that it is one informed by information." Indeed, if survival, equality, and freedom are considered as the basic values most cherished by Western civilization (Callahan, 1972), and if the problems are important enough—and we feel that those dealing with our population-environmental future are gravely so—then some attempt should be made to analyze systematically the relative orderings and tradeoffs among these values.

Another important factor (and one often misunderstood) is the difference between objectives and constraints. Very often the requirements for developing preference functions produce a meaningful differentiation between these terms. For example, three possible approaches to policy making on the yield-fertilizer problem are:

1. Maximize yield, given a constraint on the allowable ecological degradation that will be tolerated.

2. Minimize ecological damage, given a level of yield that must not be gone below.

3. Maximize an overall utility function which is constrained by fertilizer alternatives that are technologically feasible.

The first two approaches follow what is known as a "satisficing criterion," while the latter is known as "optimizing." For example, take two hypothetical alternatives to fertilizer policy concerned with short-time agricultural benefits: P_1 is the Use of Chemical Fertilizer; P_2 is the Use of Organic Fertilizer. On the basis of yield Y and ecological short-time damage D, the two policies, P_1 and P_2, are reflected in the "technological feasibilities" shown in figure 24 and in the "damage curves" shown in figure 25. Thus, P_1 is more agriculturally effective but more ecologically damaging than P_2.

When these two curves are combined, they produce a yield-damage curve, Y-D, as shown in figure 26. If it is

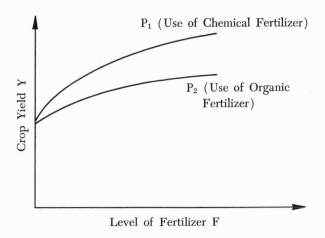

Fig. 24. Fertilizer technology curves.

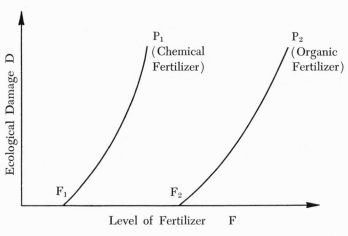

Fig. 25. Damage·curves.

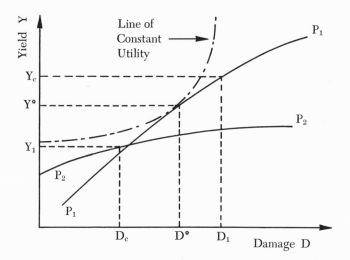

Fig. 26. Yield-damage curve.

desired to limit ecological damage to the value D_c, then policy P_2 should be used, producing yield Y_1. If a crop yield of Y_c is desired, then policy P_1 should be used, producing a level D_1 of ecological damage. If a utility structure, as sketched in figure 23, is available, then the optimal policy is P_1, producing yield Y^* and damage D^*, and the corresponding level of chemical fertilizer used can be obtained from either figure 24 or figure 25.

If a constraint is imposed upon the set of policy alternatives, an equivalent disutility is almost always associated with it. This form of analysis thus has the side benefit of allowing a systematic way of discovering which constraints are binding and what their implied marginal disutilities (shadow prices) are. In addition, the analysis again scrutinizes the sets of output variables that have been gathered together to represent the "impacts" of policy. Research into social indicators—definition and measurements—is most necessary before any such "cost-benefit" analysis can begin.

Although the rational techniques for joint (multiperson) decision making are not as promising as for individuals, the structure of the technique is important—even if it serves only as a vehicle for communication and socialization. Delphi techniques (Helmer, 1967, pp. 6–7) for eliciting group utilities could be applied to growth policy problems. Recent attempts at determining preference functions for public officials concerned with water quality (Ludlow, 1972) are a start in this direction. In addition, the concept of Pareto optimality, useful to economists in analyzing multigroup economic equilibria, is an intellectual foundation for exploring such complex issues as multinational control programs. Although the theory is by no means established (for a bibliography, see Pauly, 1967), practical applications from the consideration of disaster economics (Kunreuther, 1967) through revolts (Ireland, 1967) to voting behavior are attractive enough to be pertinent to population policy making.

One approach to an understanding of the relations in policy making between benefits (as reflected in utility for specified states of affairs) and risks (as summarized by the language of probabilities and likelihoods) is Decision Analysis (for an overview, see Howard, 1968). This uses a set of qualitative axioms set down by Von Neumann and Morgenstern (1964) that lead to an interval scale of utility encoding one's risk preferences. "Rational" decisions then follow, in the face of uncertainty, to maximize the expected (average) utility.

Although this approach has had success in a variety of situations (Brown, 1970), its adoption for public issues promises to be somewhat difficult:

The structure of the decision process—the so-called decision trees themselves may be controversial, before any consideration is even given to values or uncertainties.

Often a responsible decision maker, or policy maker, is not readily identifiable.

There is a need to establish (assign) probabilities for one-time events, a task that is formidable even for laboratory-like, repetitive events.

Multiperson problems becomes acute, even in the simplest hypothetical structures (e.g., the prisoner's dilemma) (Rapoport, 1966).

Nonetheless, because of the obviousness of the uncertainties involved in population policy, decision analysis should be brought to bear. Recent applications to the social-political-technical problems of hurricane seeding policy (Howard et al., 1972) and in medical diagnosis and treatment (Lusted, 1968; Gustavson, 1971) point the way to the use of decision analysis in aspects of macroplanning procedures. Howard's work is particularly illuminating in that it prescribes a methodology by which a public official may be brought to reveal his tradeoffs among responsibility-accepting, job-comfort, scientific advancement, and human values.

A formal procedure to lay out feelings about risk aversion and acceptance, and tradeoffs of one good for another, enables policy makers with differing views to identify points of difference as well as points of agreement. This is particularly important because some of the most difficult choices faced by society in the policy area under study involve tradeoffs between short-term and long-term benefits and risks. The traditional way of using discount rates to account for tradeoffs in time does not seem adequate with very long time horizons—that is, when the benefits of the future generations are at issue and even the survival of the entire human race is at stake. Discounting no longer seems to make sense even in a purely economic world (Meyer, 1969). This fundamental challenge to our thinking about the future value of money certainly should lead us to further study about our behavior when dealing with future value of nonmonetary goods (comfort, entertainment, children).

In particular, in the political-public environment that is the source of population policy, the relationship between the policy maker's tenure (2 to 6 years) and the time spans of the problems at hand (several generations for population to stabilize) needs to be studied. Time-trade-offs must be understood, at least within the councils of the policy makers. The social "discounting" of future goods must be considered if we are to achieve any kind of reasonable policy. In addition, the effect of expectation-reality gaps on shaping future return utilities must be studied. The motivational force supplied by expectation could be offset when past policy pronouncements are compared with their "realizations."

Are we a naturally myopic race? If we are pioneers traveling the time-line "wagon train" of Platt (1971), is it sufficient for policy makers simply to produce "maps" of costs and consequences, leaving only the traditional political process as a tool for resolving conflicts? The sense of historical process does not have equal strength among all policy makers. To what extent, therefore, is today's policy-making environment congruent with the ecosystem time frame? Will the future policy-making environment develop to make the macrosystem approach and alternative futures planning more acceptable?

Chapter VI

The Policy-Making Environment — Present and Future

It will take much time to accumulate the knowledge, develop the theory, do the research, and create the social and physical technologies appropriate for dealing with the ecosystem macroproblem. Therefore, recommendations for effective utilization of policy research in policy making must be based on assessment of the changing social and organizational context of policy making and policy research over the years ahead. In this chapter we shall examine the policy-making environment which exists today and which might develop over the next couple of decades in the United States.

It is not enough for the purposes of this discussion to assume that the policy-making process and the norms and structures that sustain it will continue to operate as they presently do. In the first place, developing and implementing and, in the light of that implementation, revising policy appropriate to the macroproblem we examine cannot be done under the processes that presently constitute what is called policy making. In the second place, there are reasons to conjecture that over the years ahead developments in society will encourage changes in the norms and processes of policy making which will make them more compatible with what seems to be required if society is to learn how to deal constructively with the macroproblem. It is important, then, to discuss the processes required for effective use of policy research, the societal conditions that will influence the processes by which policy will be created and applied, and the general organizational requirements that follow from these analyses.

Before examining aspects of these matters in more detail, it is appropriate to comment on three unavoidable characteristics of the world of policy research and policy making that presently operate and will continue to operate in the years ahead. The expression of these characteristics would change, however, if the approaches to policy making and the societal context in which policy making occurs themselves change:

1. Policy making is a social process in which intellectual input is only one component. Negotiating, bargaining, interpersonal affiliations and animosities, and personal idiosyncrasy all play, and will continue to play, critical roles (Allison, 1971).

2. Both policy research and policy making are inherently and unavoidably value-laden activities in all their aspects, as we have emphasized throughout this study.

3. For years to come there will not be an adequate scheme for systematically using policy research in policy making, although such a scheme is necessary to deal with the highly interactive societal processes. As a result, part of the task of policy making and policy research, indeed the task of society as a whole, will be *deliberately* to learn how to create, to invent, and to implement the appropriate competences and the organizational structures to sustain and reward these competencies.

Synoptic Policy Making versus
Disjointed Incrementalism

To appreciate the enormity of the task of developing a policy-making process that can deal with the macroproblem, it is necessary to distinguish between two types of policy-making as implied in previous chapters:

1. Policy arrived at through disjointed incrementalism.
2. Policy arrived at through comprehensive and strategic analysis and design ("synoptic policy making," as labeled earlier).

Studies of the policy-making process have been both descriptive and normative. Most descriptive studies have focused on the process of disjointed incrementalism because that is the way policies are typically arrived at in the United States government and, more often than commonly recognized, in corporations and third sector organizations (Bauer, 1968; Bennis, 1966; Wildavsky, 1964; Downs, 1967). As a society, we have almost no experience in synoptic policy making, certainly none appropriate to the man-environment macroproblem. Normative studies have focused on both types of policy making. What follows draws on both types of studies.

Disjointed incrementalism has developed because men and organizations have very real constraints on time, skills, resources, money, will, and power. Policy making factors distribute problems among persons and organizational components that are designed to be efficient by being specialized. In addition, much information is either unavailable or prohibitively costly to obtain. Imponderables, combined with too many alternatives to be encompassed by human minds and conjoined with value differences, result in "bounded rationality," that is, in a morass we typically deal with by norms and processes described by C. Lindblom (1965) as the method of "disjointed incrementalism."

Disjointed incrementalism as it operates, and as its proponents recommend it operate, has the following characteristics, which are extremely illuminating when contrasted to the approach we develop in this study (Lindblom and Hirschman, 1962, pp. 215–16):

1. Attempt at understanding is limited to policies that differ only incrementally from existing policy.
2. Instead of simply adjusting means to ends, ends are chosen that are appropriate to available or nearly available means.
3. A relatively small number of means (alternative possible policies) is considered, as follows from 1.
4. Instead of comparing alternative means or policies in the light of postulated ends or objectives, alternative ends or objectives are also compared in the light of postulated means or policies and their consequences.
5. Ends and means are chosen simultaneously; the choice of means does not follow the choice of ends.
6. Ends are indefinitely explored, reconsidered, discovered, rather than relatively fixed.
7. At any given analytical point ("point" refers to any one individual, group, agency, or institution), analysis and policy making are serial or successive; that is, problems are not "solved" but are repeatedly attacked.
8. Analysis and policy making are remedial; they move *away* from ills rather than *toward* known objectives.
9. At any one analytical point, the analysis of consequences is quite incomplete.
10. Analysis and policy making are socially frag-

mented; they go on at a very large number of separate points simultaneously.

Disjointed incrementalism also operates on the assumption that "in an important sense a rational problem solver wants what he can get and does not try to get what he wants except after identifying what he wants by examining what he can get" (Lindblom and Hirschman, 1962, p. 218). It accepts the policy maker as "typically a partisan, often acknowledging no responsibility to his society as a whole, frankly pursuing his own segmental interests" (p. 220). It seeks to attain sufficient comprehensiveness through a process of "*partisan* mutual adjustment" (p. 220). This process assumes that problems ignored in one policy-making decision are addressed in another. Omissions are expected to be dealt with as problems emerge, incremental policy making being seen as a serial process. Thus, rationality is recognized as an attribute of the total societal context of all policy-making decisions rather than of any particular policy-making event.

These attributes and assumptions are not adequate for the highly interactive social and ecosystem bases of the macroproblem. Instead, a comprehensive systems approach to policy making is required (Schick, 1969). No problem stands encapsulated within its definition and, hence, in its "solution"; everything reacts backward and forward on everything else. This is especially so in the hominisphere because humans react to actions not only in terms of their substantive content but also in terms of the message of intent they unavoidably convey. Events also interact over time, and policies intended to deal with the macroproblem must persist over time in forms that can be strategically and tactically adjusted in the light of changing perceptions of the goals to be valued.

Evaluation, then, is integral to policy making and so, too, is the setting of goals. Without goals as a guide there is no way to choose means strategically or to determine whether a policy is being appropriately future-responsive. Then, too, experience has demonstrated that not everyone has access to the arena of "mutual accommodation" and that goals and values about the procedures for arriving at accommodation are not sufficiently congruent to make disjointed incrementalism effective under many important circumstances (Gamson, 1968). Finally, of utmost importance, the pressing realities of the moment are not the appropriate bases either for stimulating partisan involvement or for resolving differences. Future-responsive decisions and policies designed for implementation in the present become increasingly crucial for long-range social welfare. The disjointed incremental perspectives of mutual partisan adjustment result, in the absence of future-oriented policy research, in "too little and too late," and in policies that simply are not responsive to the future.

Consequently, even though synoptic policy making enormously increases intellectual, emotional, and interpersonal burdens, we must move toward a comprehensive approach to policy making both in the analysis of a problem and in the design for dealing with it. Before describing the operational characteristics of this kind of policy making it is important to make clear that synoptic policy making as presented here also has incremental characteristics. It, too, proceeds stepwise and it never implies rigid unswerving commitment to a chosen goal and initial policy decisions for attaining it—these are always subject to review. But the incrementalism of synoptic policy making is antithetical to disjointed incrementalism. The increments involved in comprehensive policy making are guided by deliberate choices of goals, are future-oriented rather than deriving from past precedents, are innovative and implemented even though outcomes are uncertain, are articulated rather than disjointed, and are responsible and responsive to the needs of the relevant social environment (which includes other organizations), at least as much as to considerations of organizational survival and aggrandizement. As a result, the increments in synoptic policy making are likely to be "larger" in terms of alterations in concept, purpose, and action than the increments of the disjointed variety.

Probably the foremost theoretical work on comprehensive policy making is that of Yehezkel Dror (1968). He delineates the following stages in the overall comprehensive policy-making process (Dror, pp. 163–64).

The metapolicymaking stage includes seven phases:

1. Processing values
2. Processing reality
3. Processing problems
4. Surveying, processing, and developing resources
5. Designing, evaluating, and redesigning the policymaking system
6. Allocating problems, values, and resources
7. Determining policymaking strategy

The policymaking stage also happens to include seven phases:

8. Suballocating resources
9. Establishing operational goals, with some order of priority for them
10. Establishing a set of other significant values, with some order of priority for them
11. Preparing a set of major alternative policies, including some "good" ones

12. Preparing reliable predictions of the significant benefits and costs of the various alternatives

13. Comparing the predicted benefits and costs of the various alternatives and identifying the "best" ones

14. Evaluating the benefits and costs of the "best" alternatives and deciding whether they are "good" or not

The post-policymaking stage includes three phases:

15. Motivating the executing of the policy

16. Executing the policy

17. Evaluating policymaking after executing the policy

All these 17 phases are interconnected by a complex communication and feedback network, which can be considered a separate phase:

18. Communication and feedback channels interconnecting all phases

We find Dror's procedure to be quite compatible with the policy research and policy-making procedure derived in this study.

Operational variations on this approach have been proposed by Etzioni (1968, pp. 282–87) in a version he calls "mixed scanning." In this approach to policy making, policy research becomes mandatory. As Etzioni writes (1971, pp. 8–9): "Policy research is concerned with mapping alternative approaches and with specifying potential differences in the intention, effect, and cost of various programs. It differs from applied research in much the same way that strategy differs from tactics; it is more encompassing, longer-run in its perspectives, and more concerned with the goals of the unit for which it is under-taken; that is, it is more critical."

Synoptic policy making is necessary for attempting to deal with the macroproblem this study addresses; policy research is necessary to accomplish this type of policy making. This type of policy making, however, based on policy research, is not now done. To be sure, there are oc-casional studies which qualify as policy research, espe-cially some of those entombed in the appendices of Presi-dential Commission reports, but these are uncoupled both from intentions appropriate to the effort and from organizational capabilities for implementing them. De-spite much ritualistic and public relations talk about com-prehensive, farseeing policy making, in no area of the fed-eral government (with some qualified exceptions in the national security sector) is policy making comprehensive in concept, in time frame, or in organizational articula-tion. Most certainly this is true with regard to govern-ment activities substituting for comprehensive policy making in the domain of the macroproblem. Evidence for this assertion is of three sorts: (1) Documentary journal-ism, which exposes examples showing that in government offices and agencies the right hand often knows not of the left, and that different offices and agencies often are carrying out contradictory programs; (2) research, such as that conducted by authors we discuss, which invariably emphasizes this state of affairs; and (3) agency memo-randa, leaked, but not for quotation, which show that agency activities are opportunistic, responsive to White House impulse or congressional whim, or unevaluated and uncoordinated.

The utility of the type of ecosystemic policy research we propose will depend, then, on the degree to which policy makers, especially in government, move from disjointed incrementalism toward synoptic policy making in the years ahead. This movement in turn will depend upon the strength of social pressures to shift toward synoptic policy making. Although some policy makers will tend to react to these pressures by withdrawing further into disjointed incrementalism, these unprecedented pressures will create unprecedented opportunities to move toward synoptic policy making and hence toward the solicitation and use of policy research.

Anticipated Social Pressures for Facilitating Synoptic Policy Making

If these pressures develop, they will cut both ways. Under crisis conditions, members of organizations tend to retreat to modes of learned successful behavior. In most instances this means they tend to act as if they knew what to do, to become more command-oriented, to cut themselves off from new information, and to make policy exclusively by the methods of disjointed incrementalism (Janis, 1971). Their constituencies encourage such behavior by expecting them to do so. But for the first time in history the circumstances and resources for synoptic policy making will converge and thereby create unprecedented opportunities for synoptic policy making. These pressures, therefore, in part can be expected to change the perceptions and expectations of other members of organizations concerned with policy making and their relevant constituencies.

First of all, enhanced means for collecting, processing, and modeling social and ecological data will demonstrate how little we know and how inadequate are our images of the problem areas (Moynahan, 1970; Vickers, 1971). Wherever one looks today, the opinion of thoughtful experts about the status of their own field is that the more we attempt to interpret and influence the processes of society, the clearer becomes the evidence of our insufficiencies at the intellectual and operational levels (National Science Board, 1971, p. viii; Social Science Research Council, 1968–69, as quoted in Moynahan, 1970; Solo, 1972; Hertz, 1971). The following quotation, which summarizes and extends the positions of several experts in the area of information technology (Michael, *IT*, 1972, pp. 40–41) is particularly relevant here:

> Information technology, as a monitoring and guidance system, will be unavoidably immature during much of the next two decades. A crucial inhibitor will be the inadequate social technology needed to develop organizations humanely so that they can make use of information technology proportionate to its potential. Also, much of the needed data base and theory for interpreting it will still be insufficient for many applications of information technology, especially in the public interest area. Necessarily, at least the '70s will be a time for fundamental information technology—pertinent R&D on manpower, legislation, organizational design, education, ethics, as well as on information technology hardware and software *per se*.

> For organizations and for society as a whole, the impact of information technology during these decades will be sporadic, uncertain, and uneven. Information technology's development and application will be aided and obstructed by the turbulent state of the society and by the felicitous and disrupting consequences of applying immature information technology when the laws and ethics pertaining thereto are only partially developed. That is, the turbulent so-

ciety will both encourage the use of information technology to understand and guide it, and interfere with its rapid development because it will make difficult the simultaneous development of all the necessary parts of the organizational-data-hardware-legal-ethical information-decision-making system. The resultant likelihood of undesirable consequences from using only a partially developed information technology system will also discourage its application and inhibit further development if it is misapplied.

If the foregoing conjecture is even approximately valid, then the utility of technological forecasting that includes social factors (which any such forecasts must do to be truly useful) as well as future studies might seem to stand on precarious foundations indeed.

No policy research that includes reality judgments, value judgments, and instrumental judgments will be able to claim the day on intellectual grounds alone. Each model will have influence partially in terms of its intellectual appeal and partially in terms of the extent to which it meets the needs of extant policies and policy makers. A model also will have influence when it contributes to attractive myths about the nature of society and what it could become. Even disjointed incrementalists from time to time will have to use policy research to further their policy actions expediently. In some quarters, this will add legitimacy and increase attention to policy research per se. More importantly, there will be competition among policy researchers and there will be utility in "stockpiling" policy research to take advantage of "targets of opportunity" as well as to help stimulate appreciation of problem areas in need of synoptic policy making. This competitive situation will encourage policy researchers to ally themselves with offices and men in power in order to vie for ideological dominance. Thus policy researchers will be seen, and properly so, as ideologues and entrepreneurs of ideas and policy positions rather than as neutral sources of policy-relevant models and information.

In addition, policy research will become necessary as continuing increases in population size and density, resource consumption, and technology (especially in communications and transportation) result in an increasingly interactive and interdependent society. This increased density of interaction will increase the occasions when even small percentages of people and events will be socially perturbing. In turn, this will generate all kinds of social "quality-control problems" that cannot be avoided or monitored easily. Overcoming them will incur very high costs by one value criterion or another. Aircraft hijacking, oil spills, urban riots, political assassinations, and strikes by public service personnel are examples of social quality control problems, usually involving small numbers of events or people in any one locale. Policy research will be required to buttress strenuous efforts to anticipate such small percent–large impact problem situations and to monitor the socioecological settings in which they will be presumed to arise. These efforts to understand the circumstances generating the problems will engender synoptic policy-making approaches to solve them. These quality control problems also will greatly enhance the incentive to plan ahead, which, in turn, will sustain synoptic approaches.

The above developments will combine with increasing differentials in educational experience, with rising expectations, and with the trend at all levels of society toward greater expressiveness. These interactions will intensify the changing differentiation in value priorities, in social styles of expressing and demanding priorities, and in groupings around priorities and value systems (e.g., black/white, alienated/established, young/old, radical/conservative, poor/rich). Such combinations of circumstances, of course, could lead to a massive and rigid embracing of a single doctrine. If the society remains open and democratic, however, those espousing the values and operating styles of synoptic policy making will increase in numbers and influence.

These developments will lead to still more challenges to the legitimacy of organizations and conventional roles at all levels of society. This is a reflection of changing value systems and changing priorities of the U.S. It is also a result of increased public knowledge about the workings of large organizations. The challenges most frequently come from the young, but they are also evident in Congress (e.g., challenging the seniority system), among government employees (protesting the Vietnam war in defiance of the Hatch Act), in ecclesiastic hierarchies, and within corporate management. This trend will be heightened by continuing distrust of large organizations (Rotter, 1971), by the rise of a cadre of skilled advocates (whose skills in part will increase public knowledge about the duplicitous propensities of large organizations), and by increasing evidences of the inability of conventional modes of governance to deal effectively with major social and environmental issues for which they have been assigned responsibility. When failures of responsibility are recognized by constituencies, leaders and their policy-relevant methods, such as disjointed incremental policy making, will suffer further deteriorations of legitimacy.

As we postulate the macroproblem, given the high density of events and persons, the unanticipated consequences of new technologies, and the enormous burdens placed on the natural environment, social and physical crises and disasters will be a continuing condition of life. Natural disasters, when they occur, will involve more people and get more attention. The time spans of lingering "aftermaths"—of political and economic, not to say social, consequences—will be longer. Man-made disasters will evidence incompetence or lack of will on the part of policy makers. These will be ecological (e.g., deaths from inversion layers), social (e.g., assassinations or destructive confrontations), and those that are strongly socioecological (e.g., megadeaths from starvation if a blight suddenly wipes out the Green Revolution).

Disasters can be especially effective occasions for major structural and normative changes in organizations. For examples, consider the radical shift to welfare government in the United States that resulted from the disaster of the Great Depression, or the profound class changes in English society that resulted from the disaster of World War II. While such disasters can encourage Caesarism, they afford the opportunity for a revision in policy making toward a more synoptic approach, if only to improve the chances of avoiding similar disasters in the future.

Entrepreneuring policy researchers will use these disasters to keep environmental issues high on the attention scale of some segments of society and, in turn, of some policy makers. Young people, who learned to take these issues seriously during their early education, will become voters, and a new generation of administrators and professionals in government, educated in the systems approach and humanistic priorities, will come into positions of bureaucratic power. But old perspectives, greeds, indifferences, life styles, and cognitive incapacities will also persist. Conflict will intensify as evidence of the need for constraints and the costs of constraining population growth and resource consumption become clear. Adjudicating these cognitive, aesthetic, and economic differences will require far more than expediential, incremental responses. In particular, it will require attention to *future* implications as a basis for argument and assessment; this attention will further pressures and opportunities for synoptic policy making.

Revelations of such things as avoidable disasters, scandals, and exposure of attempts to cover up inadequacies in performance will persist and probably increase if society remains open. Advocates will become more skilled at disclosing and analyzing government and corporate incompetence, malpractice, and self-serving behavior. Some of the inadequacies of governance will arise from recourse to disjointed incrementalism; some from unsuccessful attempts to use synoptic policy making as the basis for decisions and actions.

Frustrations with the system and hostility toward it will persist for many or increase as a result of social "frictions" produced by conflicting incentives, goals, life styles, and value systems. These frustrations and hostilities will fuel both the exposure efforts and the intensity of styles of interpretation which overlook the dilemmas that policy makers and administrators of policies cannot avoid. Evidence of inadequacy will also be supplied by young people as well as senior government and corporate members committed to synoptic viewpoints and an environmentally enlightened perspective. A growing tendency to identify with the problem rather than the organization will encourage people more than ever to leak reports and otherwise expose the performances of those they feel are misusing the stewardship entrusted to them.

Synoptic policy-making skills, values, and motives

will be brought into organizational structures by young people. Development of these qualities more than ever will be a major educational goal of professional schools, such as engineering, public health, natural resource management, business administration, and public administration, as well as of graduate schools. They will bring much needed intellectual skills—and many will have interpersonal skills and experience useful for effective negotiation. Since some senior people also are moving toward the values and styles appropriate to synoptic policy making, certain organizations will become differentially more attractive to such young people. These organizations may succeed in producing plans and programs that are more effective and more attractive to constituents. Sometimes, they at least will convey more appealing messages of intent. Moreover, with improvements in education, there will be more people in social constituencies who will approve of efforts at synoptic policy making. Other organizations may then feel compelled to move toward synoptic policy making in order to compete for the skills of these young professionals. For reasons of intellectual limitations described earlier, initial successes in synoptic policy making will be few, while the entrenched tendencies toward disjointed incrementalism will be formidable. The existence for the first time, however, of a cadre of young people imbued with ecosystemic reality and value images, and trained in synoptic policy research and policy making, will provide a thrust where none existed previously.

Resistance and Transition to Synoptic Policy Making

As the needs and opportunities for synoptic policy making emerge, encouraged by the circumstances just reviewed, there will be much to be learned about how to introduce such a significantly different policy approach. Effective implementation will require continuing interaction between policy researchers and policy makers, in itself an innovation we must learn to effectuate. This learning process will involve overcoming organizational barriers to the reception of relevant information, developing special interpersonal capabilities, and encouraging policy-relevant research in new areas.

Organizations have great difficulty soliciting and using information that might upset the internal status quo. This has been especially but not uniquely true in government. In corporations, the compelling threat of competition sometimes produces sensitivity to indicators of profit and loss, market share, and so forth. But even corporations strongly resist information that would require shifts in policy or perspective. These barriers to the collection and use of upsetting information contribute to the "rationality" of disjointed incrementalism and help to sustain its processes (Rehfus, 1972).

The causes of such barriers may be psychological, organizational, or mechanical. Psychological barriers arise from the interplay of social and emotional factors. They include general barriers to human communication as well as those specifically applicable to governmental decision making. Organizational barriers are related to organizational character and structure, and the ways in which organizations screen out information. This screening may be internal, creating barriers within the organization, or external, creating barriers between organizations and their clients. Mechanical barriers result from sheer volume of information and from the physical or economic difficulties of collection, processing, and dissemination. (Government studies of information transfer usually deal with this type of barrier, and then only with regard to factual information [NSF, 1964]).

Many psychological barriers result from our unwillingness or inability to live with high levels of uncertainty. Donald Schon, following Frank Knight, has usefully distinguished between risk and uncertainty (Schon, 1967). Risk pertains when one thinks one knows the variables in a situation. Thereby, one feels able to assign probabilities to the influence and interaction of these variables on outcomes. Uncertainty pertains when one feels one has either too much or too little information to know what are the relevant variables, i.e., one knows one doesn't know. This psychological uncertainty is to be distinguished from uncertainty as defined in decision analysis or economics. Psychological uncertainty generates anxiety because it carries the threat of losing control of a situation or of being caught in an error.

Psychological uncertainty leads persons such as would-be policy makers to do what they can, usually unconsciously, to avoid information that would add to their sense of uncertainty. They do this by many strategies: by being unwilling to recognize or admit the need for new information, by avoiding information sources (especially policy research) which might contradict established positions, and by avoiding exposure to sources of information which could suggest that controversial or unorthodox positions may be valid. These strategies are reinforced by the deep-seated tendency to perceive only that which is consistent with what we already believe or "know," by our tendency to avoid emotional upset, and by interpersonal processes emphasizing cohesion which operate in any enduring small group (Miller and Rice, 1967). Together, these tendencies serve to maintain group intra-dependencies at the expense of innovative attention to problems if the shared images of the group are threatened by the innovation.

The most frequent avoidance tactics are those that emphasize inside expertise, minimize feedback from the outside, and use outside expertise that has proved itself compatible with the ongoing processes of the organization. Of course, there are exceptions to all of these uncertainty-avoiding actions. Sometimes new senior personnel bring in their own novel ideas, sometimes feedback is successfully forced on the organization from outside, and sometimes "reliable" consultants have or develop "hidden agendas." For reasons described earlier, these exceptions can be expected to increase. The overwhelming tendency of people in organizations is to act to avoid psychological uncertainty. The conditions for moving them and their organizations permanently away from information-avoiding strategies will be difficult to attain.

The link between psychological resistances to using new upsetting information and the organizational barriers to doing so is established by Rehfus (1972, p. 9): "Information input from accepted sources is converted into organizational policy; policy or decisions thus made shape the organizational character, making future information from the same source fit neatly into the established patterns of the organization; so in the future more information is sought from these sources because it conforms so well to the 'needs' of the organization as perceived by those people in it."

Several kinds of organizational barriers are worth specific attention, in addition to endemic resort to disjointed incrementalism, which by its very nature minimizes the need for or attention to novel information. Three properties of most organizations in their own right

contribute to the erection of substantial information barriers as well as encouraging disjointed incrementalism,
Wilensky (1967, pp. 43 ff.) describes them as hierarchy,
specialization, and centralization. These properties typify
bureaucracies, certainly at the federal level where synoptic
policy making most often should occur.

The steeply pyramidal structure of hierarchy makes
possible centralization and unity of command, but it invariably leads to distortions and dilutions of communications both upward and downward (Likert, 1961). A major
contribution comes from ambitious and upwardly mobile
subordinates who distort and block information:

> Men on their way up were prone to restrict informa-
> tion about such issues as lack of authority to meet re-
> sponsibilities, fights with other units, unforeseen costs,
> scheduling of work flow, fruitless progress reports,
> constant interruptions, insufficient time or budget to
> train subordinates, insufficient equipment or sup-
> plies, and so on. Restriction of such problem informa-
> tion is motivated by the desires not only to please
> but also to preserve comfortable routines of work
> (Wilensky, 1967, p. 43).

Officials may distort the information flow upward in several ways: (1) minimizing or suppressing information un-
favorable to them; (2) exaggerating information favorable
to them; and (3) selecting information to pass upward
that will suggest continuation of present policies or expenditure of more resources on their programs. The effects on policy makers at the top levels in government
agencies and bureaus of this kind of selection and distortion are predictable. Fearing they are being deceived or
kept in the dark, they begin to emphasize loyalty indoctrination, and other methods that tend to create "organi-

zation men." This in turn creates new barriers to communication of information, so fewer new ideas and critical questions than ever find their way to the top.

Specialization tends to encourage rivalry and further restrict the flow of information. The presence of specialists and special functions creates areas of knowledge not accessible to others without the active cooperation of the specialized source, which is motivated to protect its special functions by withholding information. Information of this nature could be used to persuade and facilitate accommodation with rivals. Instead, this information often is kept for selective release when it will be of value to the organization in a struggle for power, position, or budgetary advantage.

Centralization presents its own dilemma, the typical "resolution" of which results in barriers to effective information intake and utilization. If information input is too close to top management or government policy makers, a few select officials and experts are overloaded with information, and hard put to use it effectively. If information input is lower in the hierarchy and scattered throughout subordinate units, the problems of specialization and the withholding or distortion of information for strategic use occur.

Mechanical barriers are worth distinguishing from psychological and organizational barriers, although to a substantial degree they are themselves the product of reluctance to use or seek new information; the technological and intellectual resources needed to reduce this barrier are available but unapplied. Mechanical barriers to the use of information are: (1) the information is not "digested" and displayed in useful ways; (2) the information is not translated into terms useful for the policy maker; and (3) too much time was spent in inefficient processing of the information, or too little money was spent to permit efficient processing, to leave time enough for the information to be influential in policy making. As a result of such mechanical barriers the potential user of policy research can be overloaded to the point that essentially only information compatible with his preconceptions gets attended to. Robert Biller (1969, p. 6) emphasizes this source of overload: "the current idea, 'rationality results from minimizing the costs of information,' should be replaced with 'rationality results from minimizing the risks of information unavailability.'"

It will be extremely difficult to overcome these mechanical barriers to the solicitation and use of information that effective policy research should make available. Limited funds, time, manpower, skills, and technology as well as contradictory and constricting statutes, mandates, prerogatives, and directives reinforce the barriers. Removing administrative, legal, economic, mechanical, and political constraints would significantly improve the chances for transition toward synoptic policy making. These constraints persist, however, because removing them would face policy makers with the private and public costs of coping with innovation. Such revisions require extremely difficult adjustments in fundamental reality and value images.

Fundamentally, this would mean making changes in oneself. Thus, a necessary but not sufficient condition for synoptic policy making in the turbulent situation of the next two decades will be the development of specific personal and interpersonal capabilities in policy makers as well as policy researchers. They must acquire the will and skill to overcome the barriers to effective information utilization.

Policy makers and policy researchers will have to acknowledge particularly high levels of psychological uncertainty. To be sure, in some situations policy research, using analytical procedures such as those suggested in chapter 5, will reduce uncertainty. More often than not, however, a strong incentive to look more certain than the situation merits will lead policy makers to commit themselves and their organizations to one or another model and the reality images inherent in it—if indeed they do not retreat to disjointed incrementalism. Corresponding incentive will lead policy researchers to reduce their own uncertainties by claiming more for their model or proposals than justified, or by allowing themselves to be co-opted by powerful men and agencies to gain comfort in times of uncertainty by association with power and influence (Michael, 1968). Since our culture bestows leadership on those who project certainty, one's self-image and one's public image depend on avoidance of uncertainty; one does this either by neglecting information that produces uncertainty or by gratuitously treating it as risk. "Government policy making presently has a tendency to delay for a long time the introduction of a new program because of uncertainties and then suddenly to jump in fully with a large commitment to a prescribed program, with no better knowledge base than before, when political pressures for doing something became strong. Once proposed or initiated, the program is then popularized among the public and in the Congress as a sure antidote, rather than as a promising probe of the environment" (Nelson et al., 1967, pp. 173–74). Overcoming personal and social compulsions to avoid uncertainty will be as difficult as it will be necessary. But, as we shall discuss later, it will not be impossible for some people.

The first step in overcoming this compulsion is to learn to make constructive use of error. The period ahead must be treated as a context in which to learn *how* to do synoptic policy making and how to produce the ideas and information that facilitate it. Not having learned how to do it, we will make many errors. Men and institutions will need to treat error as the explicit basis for learning how to do synoptic policy making rather than to deny its existence or blame others when they make errors. At present, men and institutions have deeply embedded motives for obscuring the fact of error and for acting in ways that minimize the risk of error. Attempts at synoptic policy making, however, will contain a high likelihood of error. High probabilities of error will seem more evident than the low risks of error presumed inherent in disjointed incrementalism—low risks which have added up to the monumental macroproblem we now must face. In order to learn how to use policy research and thereby do better synoptic policy making, it will be necessary to make the very difficult shift from a personal and organizational mode of error-denying and error-burying to one of error-embracing. The rewards will have to go to those men and organizations who structure their researches and policies so that their errors can be discovered and used to improve understanding and subsequent policy making.

Rather than move away from the past in a disjointed fashion, synoptic policy planning would move toward desired alternative futures with due appreciation of the systemic benefits and costs involved in alternative goal choices. Goal setting cannot be avoided when the policy making task is to deal with systems problems whose conditions for resolution must be located in the future. But goal setting is fraught with deep intellectual and emotional difficulties because such choices always involve value priorities. That is why, under disjointed incrementalism, one agrees on means which can operate in furtherance of more than one goal, goals about which there may be no consensus. But, as the future will reveal ever more clearly, means have consequences as well and contain goals which, through synergistic interaction, may exacerbate the situation.

Goal setting in synoptic policy making should result in policy guides and stimuli, not rigid endpoints to be pursued without evaluation or revision. The task of policy research is to aid in the creation of the means for moving toward them. But the action of goal setting enlarges the realm of uncertainty, increases the chances of being caught out in error later, and exposes the participants to the dread of dealing with their own strong feelings and those of others. In this society, we try to "keep feelings out of rational behavior" at demonstrably great cost to effective operations (Bennis, 1966; Argyris, 1969; Miller and Rice, 1967). Yet research on organizational behavior makes it clear that feelings are believed to reduce efficiency and rationality, to be unmanly, and to be too impolite to express in decision-making activities. As a result, we have a learned incapacity for dealing constructively with strong feelings in ourselves and in others. Nevertheless, if synoptic policy making is to be undertaken, policy makers and policy researchers will have to develop skills in accepting and constructively dealing with strong and often conflicting feelings among those participating in goal setting activities.

Along with overcoming tendencies to avoid uncertainties, effective feedback of information must become available. As the discussion on barriers to information utilization stressed, there is much resistance to seeking and accepting new information. The literature on organizational behavior emphasizes that a chief means of avoiding such information is to minimize contacts with the relevant environments by not soliciting feedback or by restricting the means to messages that tend to reinforce the conventional activities and viewpoints of the organization (Wilensky, 1967; Downs, 1967; Webb, 1969; Rosenthal and Weiss, 1966). There are also ubiquitous means for avoiding the use of feedback information. Organizations can be structured to encapsulate incoming messages in particular subdivisions of the organization, where they die. Organizations can diffuse the information so that it takes too much effort to bring it together for policy making. They also buck it up to the top, where it is disposed of in ways that protect the self images and previous commitments of senior personnel. Much information generated by policy research, especially that oriented to the future, disappears for these reasons.

Synoptic policy making requires active solicitation and use of feedback. Given the world projected earlier, feedback will be forced on organizations, especially governmental, by active and skilled advocates to a degree never before experienced. Thus, feedback will carry threats of: increased uncertainty; exposure to errors through evaluation; and review and revision of goals and programs (and thereby the threat of reorganizing and dissolving groupings of people who will have looked to each other for psychological strength, especially in turbulent times). Both fundamental structural and social psychological changes will be required.

As the environment for policy research and policy making undergoes these fundamental changes and presumably becomes more conducive to synoptic policy making, new and larger sources of policy research funding will emerge. As evidence accumulates that the macroproblem cannot be managed by disjointed and incremental efforts, and as professionals and their constituencies ask new kinds of questions, there will be a growing acknowledgment that synoptic policy making is a necessary and effective approach. This will increase the requests for comprehensive policy research. Already this is evident in such Congressional efforts as the bill to establish a technology assessment capability. Outside government, it is evident in the substantial policy and protopolicy research carried out by such groups as the Federation of American Scientists, Common Cause, the Center for a Voluntary Society, the Club of Rome, and the various groups associated with Ralph Nader. In addition, recent presidential commissions have often willfully overstepped the intentions of an administration by approaching their tasks in the spirit of policy research rather than of applied research, usually to the annoyance of the administration. (For example, the commissions on urban disturbances, violence, pornography, marijuana, and to some degree the Commission on Population Growth and the American Future.) Even if government agencies at first are reluctant to make funds available for policy research and to create the structures to apply it, extragovernmental agencies will do so. This ultimately will force government offices to respond in kind, if only in self-defense. Whether they then will use that research in a context that meets the social psychological requirements for overcoming barriers to the use of new information remains to be seen.

The synoptic policy research that emerges will have to open up new areas of research that are presently taboo. This research will have to question basic value premises about the appropriate conduct of people and to explore policy alternatives not easily made compatible with concepts of private property, private and public growth in material matters, economic regulation, personal choice of family size, etc. It is one thing to support such studies in the manner of commission. It is quite another for a particular agency to use public funds to support intensive research intended to be *applied* to policy making. For example, there is now a law that prohibits the study of the behavior of juries through direct observation.

Perhaps the most delicate research area that will have to receive much more attention will be that of intensive study of the social psychology of the policy-making process itself. This research will be for the purposes of changing that social psychology in order to increase the ability of the policy maker to use policy research. Such studies, of course, will require that policy makers expose themselves to studies. Research on how and on what to establish government policy regarding policy-making processes for effective governance also must be undertaken. Until it is, it will be virtually impossible for our society to take adequate advantage of the pressures and opportunities for synoptic policy making.

Organizational Redesign to Facilitate Synoptic Policy Making

A major task for those who would do synoptic policy making in the years ahead, and for those who would do the research upon which to base it, will be to discover new organizational arrangements to facilitate it. We have discussed requirements for taking advantage of forces providing occasions for developing synoptic policy-making procedures. These requirements in turn suggest some recommendations for organizational redesign to utilize policy research in policy making. These recommendations must be modest because there does not now exist a technology of organizational design that would specify how to arrange the internal structure of organizations and relationships among them if synoptic policy making were to be the norm (Michael, 1972; Argyris, 1972). Certainly there is nothing to guide us when the picture of policy-making procedures will be a mixed one, as it doubtless will be over the next couple of decades.

Thus, at this point the most we can usefully recommend are structural and personal changes to facilitate the learning processes which must occur before and in order that significant organizational redesigns may be accomplished. This learning process will be a continuing process, and one that of itself will generate much uncertainty. The task has a magnitude commensurate with that of the synoptic macrosystem policy-making approach we outline in this study. First of all there is a need to change norms in organizations in order to support uncertainty acknowledgment, error embracing, goal setting, and feedback soliciting. While these changes would modify the modes of accountability, responsibility, and authority, they would not eliminate them. Nor would they eliminate the presence of power or the need for negotiation. These changes, however, would alter the conditions and norms under which power is used and negotiation undertaken (Michael, 1972). Such changes, therefore, at the minimum would require revision of personal and interpersonal competences and of organizational structure. There would have to be changes in laws and statutes, and in public expectancies about how policy making should be done. The emerging conditions could facilitate social support for such changes.

Some of the structural changes suggested in various studies to facilitate synoptic policy making are especially relevant. Eugene J. Webb, after analyzing why it is that organizations do not use the information available to them (Webb, 1969, pp. 39–40), turns to David Bobrow's recommendations for improving the situation. He observes that Bobrow suggests the following:

Problems associated with biases of individuals

1. Problem: Tendencies to modify information in order to protect from and ingratiate with superiors and peers.

   Remedy: Assign use of information system to persons who are: (1) professionally not dependent on superiors; (2) characterized by low needs for group approval; (3) attached to reference groups which esteem nondistorting use of the information system; (4) members of organizations which are in fact (and in principle) charged with reporting *bad* as well as good news; (5) in contact with and under the partial protection of alternative authority figures.

2. Problem: Tendencies to modify information to protect favored programs.

   Remedy: Assign indicator system to persons and organizations which have no direct responsibility for developing or managing particular programs.

3. Problem: Tendencies to fit indicator system to previous cognitions and effects.

   Remedy: Assign indicator system to persons and organizations which are: (1) diverse in the previous cognitions and effects represented; (2) aware of the conservative biasing tendencies of all persons; (3) in frank and frequent communication with persons and groups with diverse memories and world-views.

4. Problem: Tendencies to ignore information about long-range effects beyond tenure in role.

   Remedy: Assign indicator system to persons with career commitment to problem as distinct from particular organization or policy.

Problems associated with biases from organization characteristics

At least the following sources of organizational distortion should be taken into account:

1. Problem: Tendencies to act parochially toward an information system—considering only aspects relevant to a portion of the full set of potential uses of the system.

   Remedy: Assign indicator system to organization: (1) whose members do not view organizational survival as depending on reaching a particular small goal using particular methods to reach goals; (2) whose mission is a total analysis of the large problem area rather than of some small group of programs; (3) which does not have a clientele whose interests are better served by a particular and prespecifiable set of goals and methods by others.

2. Problem: Tendencies to select information (before it reaches decision centers) to fit with organizational growth, style, and reputation.

Remedy: Assign indicator system to organization: (1) which has little hierarchy and reports directly to highest relevant decision maker; (2) which has not aged to the point of evolving a uniform, constraining set of internal norms; (3) which develops a sampling plan for behavior that evidences the state of affairs.

Harold Wilensky also makes a number of detailed recommendations for organizational readjustments (1967, pp. 175–78). The following are selected from his chart, "Roots of Intelligence Failure, Typical Effects, and Organizational Defenses":

Roots of Failure: Structural attributes that maximize distortion and blockage

Many ranks in hierarchy, emphasis on rank in style and symbolism. A tall pyramid narrowing sharply at the top, providing long promotion ladders for a few.

Main Effects on Intelligence:
Blocks upward communication. More effort to create organization men via loyalty criteria in recruitment, indoctrination, etc. Keeps experts in their "place" (subordinate, isolated). (But hierarchy eases internal control, motivates hard work.)

Organizational Defenses Against Information Pathologies:

Team or project organization. Investigation and inspection machinery. Communicate out of channels. Rely on informed outsiders. Diversify channels. Develop general advisers at the top. Accent persuasion, manipulation in administrative style.

Roots of Failure: "Intelligence" ("information gathering" or "research") vs. "operations" (clandestine operations).

Main Effects on Intelligence:

Fact-gathering attracts naive realists with weak interpretive abilities. Secret operations attract adventurer unreliable, hard to control.

Organizational Defense Against Information Pathologies:

Integrate research and operations. Accent research. Rotation. Make secret agencies accountable to competent (strong, independent) authority. Restrict clandestine action.

Roots of Failure: Prediction or estimate vs. analysis and orientation.

Main Effects on Intelligence:

Prediction inappropriate where identity of enemy is unclear, organizational goals ambiguous or conflicting, policy alternatives poorly defined. Boss asks the impossible, expert wastes time. Demand for short, speedy journalistic estimates of future diverts experts from proper work. Failure of short-run predictions reinforces anti-intellectualism. "Cry wolf syndrome."

Organizational Defense Against Information Pathologies:

Train executives in uses and limits of experts in various fields. Recruit better-trained experts, who will limit claims and maintain professional autonomy. Invest more in general orienting analyses.

When structural changes are attempted, improvements in personal and interpersonal skills will have to occur before the changes are accepted and used as intended. Accepting the structural innovations in organizational arrangements suggested above will require overcoming strong resistances to change in organizational norms and standards. Developing a capacity to face oneself and others constructively so that intense uncertainty can be acknowledged, error embraced, and strong feelings engaged openly will require the cultivation of a sense of self and of ways to relate to others quite different from those conventionally experienced.

To help persons adapt to change, certain planned social change techniques have been developed, usually associated with what is called "organizational development." These techniques, while still immature, have been applied with some significant success to the redesign of organizations and to the improvement of self understanding and interpersonal skills (Likert, 1967; Marrow, et al., 1967; Bennis et al., 1969; Havelock, 1971; and others). Although few applications have been made to government, civil servants are increasingly exposed to the ideas in seminars conducted by the Civil Service Commission. Some distinguished business schools now train their students in the theory and practice of these methods. All indications are that the organizational development approach will spread, especially because some corporations find it valuable and that alone will help legitimize it. Some of the techniques used for organizational development are: Sensitivity Training Group, Reflection, Authentic Feedback, Role Playing, Group Observation and Process Analysis, Gaming, The Derivative Conference, Survey Feedback, Brainstorming, and Synectics. (Aspects of role playing were discussed as Gaming Simulation in chapter 5.)

Experience with corporations and voluntary organizations makes it clear that any substantial effort at reconstruction takes at least from three to five years. Furthermore, organizational development will only work if senior personnel are thoroughly involved as direct participants in the experience. Naturally, this exposes them to anxious and unfamiliar experiences. But evidence from other situations indicates they can cope with this experience if they believe their organization's competence depends on accomplishing such alterations. If senior people are not full participants, the message is clear to those who are risking changing themselves, by exposing themselves to organizational development experiences, that either nothing will change or that the new ways of behaving will not apply at the top levels. Either way, this makes a ritual of the activity, which thereby fails to eliminate and actually increases distrust and behavior aimed at the avoidance of uncertainty and error.

At present, commitment from the top is especially difficult to obtain in government. If these circumstances persist, then the prerequisites for synoptic policy making cannot be met. There is good reason to believe, however, that present circumstances cannot and will not persist, at least not as ubiquitously as they do now.

Much research and development are needed to learn

the limits and possibilities of these techniques. Those seeking to further the application of policy research must see as a crucial part of that purpose the fostering of research on organizational development.

Organizational development is a necessary prelude to setting up an organizational situation in which policy research will be used. Once a sympathetic set of organizational structures, norms, and interpersonal skills is available, there is still the task of insuring that policy researchers and policy makers are related in ways that maximize their mutual utility. The most elaborate survey of the field of knowledge utilization in relation to innovation identifies three basic orientations toward that task and concludes that application should be determined by each particular mix of circumstances, knowledge, recipients, and purposes (Havelock, 1971). Thus, it is not meaningful here to recommend a particular strategy with regard to the use of knowledge created from macrosystems policy research. But it is useful to describe the three orientations for what they imply about allocation of organizational effort and organizational design—about how large an investment must be made in reconstructing an activity whose nature and dynamics are usually taken for granted. Havelock identifies the three orientations as: (1) The Problem-Solving Strategic Orientation; (2) the Social Interaction Strategic Orientation; and (3) the Research, Development, and Diffusion Strategic Orientation, and in his discussion (Havelock, pp. 2–14) explains as follows:

1. The Problem-Solving Strategic Orientation

This orientation rests on the primary assumption that innovation is a part of a problem-solving process which goes on inside the user. Problem solving is usually seen as a patterned sequence of activities beginning with a *need*, sensed and articulated by the client, which is translated into a *problem* statement and *diagnosis*. When he has thus formulated a problem statement, the client-user is able to conduct a meaningful *search* and *retrieval* of ideas and information which can be used in formulating or selecting the *innovation*. Finally, the user needs to concern himself with *adapting* the innovation, *trying out* and *evaluating* its effectiveness in *satisfying* his original need. The focus of this orientation is the user, himself, his needs and what he does about satisfying his needs. The role of outsiders is therefore consultative or collaborative. . . .

2. The Social Interaction Strategic Orientation

A second strategic orientation places emphasis on the patterns by which innovations diffuse through a social system. This perspective . . . views the innovation as something relatively fixed and concrete. . . . Usually the "innovation" is a concrete item such as a fertilizer, a new kind of seed, a new drug, or a new curriculum package.

3. The Research, Development, and Diffusion Strategic Orientation

. . . This orientation is guided by at least five assumptions. First, it assumes that there should be a *rational sequence* in the evolution and application of an innovation. This sequence should include research, development, and packaging before mass dissemination takes place. Second, it assumes that there has to be planning, usually on a massive scale over a long time span. Third, it assumes that there has to be a *division and coordination of labor* to accord with the rational sequence and the planning. Fourth, it makes the assumption of a more-or-less *passive but rational consumer* who *will* accept and adopt the innovation if it is offered to him in the right place at the right time and in the right form. Fifth and finally, proponents . . . accept the fact of high initial development cost prior to any dissemination activity because of the anticipated long-term benefits in *efficiency* and *quality* of the innovation and its suitability for mass audience dissemination.

Prototypes of this RD&D model are presumed to exist in industry and agriculture.

Each orientation has a strategy and tactics associated with it. To use these effectively will take deliberate effort and planning rather than the casual and almost invariably ineffective approaches presently resorted to. Deliberate attention to the linkage between knowledge research and knowledge utilization strongly suggests the need for specific organizational activities, sometimes for specific organizations, devoted to this task. As Havelock and other students of these processes emphasize (e.g., Rogers and Shoemaker, 1971) research and development are needed in this area as well. To fund policy research and be indifferent to the need to fund research on methods for efficiently linking new knowledge with its users would be self-defeating.

Personal and organizational changes and subsequent attention to linking policy research with policy making need to be accompanied by an enlargement and involvement of the policy constituencies. Obviously, dealing with the macroproblem of population and the environment will require the coordination or integration of many discrete organizational policies. This of itself will require moving as many relevant organizations as possible in the direction of synoptic policy making. At this point it will be vitally necessary for government organizations to establish arrangements to ensure that policy-relevant research is disseminated to organizations *outside* the government so they may contribute effectively to the synoptic policy-making process. The public will need to support synoptic policy making and become involved in the policy making as well as policy research stages.

This experimental approach to learning how to deal with the macroproblem of population and the environment asks that policy makers acknowledge uncertainty, embrace error, and set goals as points of reference rather than as rigid targets. For them to do so will require constituencies who will support them. If publics persist in expecting government leadership to act as if it really knew what it was doing, to act to maximize present satisfactions while leaving the future to chance, to act as if to acknowledge error is to acknowledge inadequacy, then no policy maker seeking to move toward synoptic policy making will survive. These constituencies themselves must readjust their images. They will have to understand the nature of the problems faced and will have to accept the performance norms appropriate for synoptic policy making. This at a minimum will require public access to the same knowledge and data the policy makers use. In addition, this implies the opportunity for the public to evaluate the data and propose alternative policies. Much research and field experience emphasizes that public participation is a critical prerequisite for active support. Out of participation comes the understanding—reality, judgmental, and instrumental—of the problem, of the values involved, and of the political and organizational constraints that so fundamentally affect the potentiality of any policy.

Initial public support must be followed up by ensuring knowledgeable feedback to and from the relevant constituencies so they can monitor the synoptic policy-making processes and the consequences of policy decisions. The macroproblem of population and the environment involves issues so complex and interorganizational relationships so elaborate that the involved bureaucracies might cut themselves off, deliberately or inadvertently, from public access. To be sure, this familiar bureaucratic tendency would be less under the social psychological conditions required for synoptic policy making. During the next two decades there certainly will be many incentives for bureaucracies to set up barriers against "meddling" and "carping" from the outside—if only to reduce what are certain to be exceedingly heavy information overloads. One of the most effective ways government agencies can "protect themselves from protecting themselves" will be to ensure that competent critics and supporters outside the government have access to the policy research on which they are basing their proposals (Michael, 1970). To provide this access will complicate the policy-making process, and could even destroy the possibilities of making synoptic policies in some situations. This is a risk a democracy must face as it tries to learn how to be a democracy in the world of the macroproblem. After all, the present form of governance has taken 200 years of experimenting, and we are still experimenting via the eighteen-year-old vote. There seems to be no way out of this difficulty. Our survival will depend on something other than disjointed incrementalism and the public expectancies associated with that style of stumbling backward into the future.

Even informing and communicating with the public may not be sufficient conditions for survival. There is need to increase the likelihood that additional concepts and alternatives be made available for policy making beyond those supplied at any given time by the institutionalized policy research community. While there will be variety in what is produced by policy research, strong forces will constrain that variety. Both researchers and policy-making consumers will tend to reinforce whatever ideas are in good currency at a given time. Funds and prestige will reward policy researchers whose beliefs and techniques are compatible with the beliefs and needs of policy makers. To a lesser but substantial degree, this process works in reverse as well. Policy makers will want to be identified with the ideas and techniques of prestigious and "in" policy researchers. Furthermore, the perspectives of both groups will inevitably be filtered by their experiences, intentions, and organizational settings (Warwick, 1971). Ideas and alternatives produced by groups outside this rather closed loop of reality, value, and instrumental judgments are likely to be different in important ways, not the least of which will be differences in images and perspectives—as organizations have been learning when they listen to the poor, women, students, homosexuals, and others. As established organizations are beginning to realize, the confrontation between different perspectives can often lead to new social inventions and arrangements that are productive and rewarding for all. The same can be expected with regard to "outside" responses to policy research information. Outside groups will expand on this information, reject some of it, and create unexpected interpretations and proposals from it.

To develop an effective macrosystem policy-making approach will require a degree of public support heretofore not envisioned. For the sake of public support, bureaucratic responsiveness, and conceptual vitality, it will be incumbent on organizations to arrange their operations to ensure the distribution of policy research findings and resources to potential supporters and critics outside their boundaries. In view of the worldwide scope of the man-environment macroproblem, arrangements to do this will have to propagate, in turn, regional, international, and global organizations.

Chapter VII

The Interdependency of National and Global Growth Policies

Although at the outset we established our concern for the *world* macroproblem, in developing a macrosystem approach and considering a policy-making process we focused on the United States because of our relative familiarity with its situation. At the same time the macroproblem and even its partial solutions are not restricted to any single country in the world. A macrosystem approach to policy making and the policy-making environment in which it is applicable ideally should be extended to include international and global considerations. When such extensions are made, further problems arise.

From the standpoint of policy making in general, the world is presumed to have some 150 sovereign countries. In actuality, some of these countries are composed of such heterogeneous groups—ethnic, regional, socioeconomic, and so forth—that their policies often are less consistent and less representative of their constituencies than those of a bloc of countries which happen to be more homogeneous in certain aspects of their images and therefore in their corresponding policies. For instance, in many of the recent debates on the environmental issues intimately related to industrial growth, the contrasting views are those of the industrialized, developed countries and those of the less-developed countries. Although this simplistic contrast ignores many differences within each of these two groups of countries, as well as the transition of countries into the industrialized group, the contrast can help identify the issues related to the impact of industrial growth on the world's resources and on ecosystem Earth.

Numerous articles have pointed out that the most industrialized country, the United States, with only about 6 percent of the world's population, annually consumes about 30 percent of the world's nonrenewable resources. With the less-developed countries undergoing "the great ascent" toward a much improved material standard of living (Heilbroner, 1963), there is now a demand for an international accounting of natural resource usage. Increasing the price of imports (raw materials, petroleum, etc.) will affect the pattern of United States economic and industrial growth. The extent of the impact is difficult to predict, because the long-run shifting needs of the other countries have not been projected and evaluated in terms of known resource reserves, which in addition change with technological development and new discoveries.

The exchange of natural resources is one of many exchanges among nations that affect their growth patterns and consequent ecosystem impacts. Other important exchanges include manufactured goods (both capital and consumption), technology, information, and even sociocultural values and fundamental image experiences. The "exchange of population," migration, can be expected to continue to be limited in spite of the trend toward more liberal immigration policies in various countries. Nevertheless, migration is stimulated by the organization of socioeconomic blocs such as the European Economic Community, which has been a conscious historical force working to facilitate international integration.

International interaction goes beyond exchanges. Environmental pollution respects no national boundaries and illustrates a set of problems that will require international solutions (Russell and Landsberg, 1971). The MIT/SCEP report (1970) cites a number of these environmental problems of global scope (e.g., CO_2, DDT, etc.). However, the ecosystem impacts of both the simple interactions and the synergisms among population size, population distribution, resource consumption, and technological development hardly have been studied at the international level. (A significant and much needed contribution in this area is Caldwell, 1972.) The basic macro-system procedures for studying the policy process should be applicable within and among all countries, although specific adaptations will have to be worked out to make the procedures operational at the international level.

The 1972 United Nations Stockholm Conference on the Human Environment indicated reservations on environmental issues by the less-developed countries. Little mention was made about the sensitive issue of unabated population growth. In countries undergoing industrialization, the migration of farmers into urban areas, often slums, accompanies the increase of pollution in the industrialized zones, phenomena that have often gone hand in hand with the growth of GNP. Ironically, many less-developed countries de-emphasize pollution, or even "import pollution in order to achieve economic growth," although a large portion of their citizens sustain themselves by direct contact with the polluted environment (e.g., drinking, bathing, laundering, and subsistence fishing in rivers into which industry and communities discharge their wastes). Another dilemma faced by some countries undergoing industrialization is that while GNP increases with industrialization, unemployment of unskilled labor displaced by mechanization also increases, at least during a transition period. The critical question of more growth or more employment in some of the less-developed countries (Chandavarkar, 1972) makes poignant the issue of rapid economic growth *versus* socially acceptable distribution of income.

Of course, in any hierarchy of needs, getting enough food and shelter for survival initially is more important than keeping a clean and pleasing environment. But is this the choice less-developed countries are forced to make? Cannot policy research identify other options? Take the policy of technological transfer, for example. Too often a less-developed country will decide to import a technology from an industrialized nation without consideration of environmental compatibility. Despite the availability of a range of technological options, the technology to be imported may be far from the best for the local economic, social, and natural environment, usually characterized by a surplus of low-skilled labor, a shortage of maintenance technicians, a shortage of capital and foreign exchange, and a concentration of people in urban areas. The less-developed countries need to be concerned for and capable of technology assessment. For the same reason, the donor country needs to be wary about including its own equipment and technology in its package of bilateral aid. These force a technological choice, purposefully or inadvertently, which often defeats the long-run intent of the aid.

For example, the Green Revolution quickly increased the yield of agricultural output. At the same time it also increased both local unemployment and the long-term vulnerability of agricultural production by encouraging monocultures. What has become clear is that in some countries, simple rototillers may be more desirable for farming than tractors. Policy research should determine at what point the Green Revolution becomes a disservice to a specific country. The research also should identify the other sociotechnological programs which should be implemented along with an agricultural revolution in order to create a desirable total package for achieving national goals.

Although different countries set their various goals by different processes, no country can grow substantially in isolation from the rest of the world. If a country grows exponentially in population or use of natural resources, or seriously disrupts natural ecosystem linkages, it will come into conflict with other countries long before encountering ecosystem limits. World history in part consists of struggles among nations competing for natural resources, but now the specter of thermonuclear war and the worldwide awareness of the precariousness of the ecosphere make it clear that no country can afford to set its growth policy arbitrarily or unilaterally.

There are no effective international organizations for conflict resolution or global policy making (although there are many helpful international agencies) and there is no truly enforceable international legal system. However, the world so far has managed to avoid a thermonuclear war, and tension between the superpowers may be lessening. This suggests that the kind of interdependent decision logic used in arms control might be useful until a better system for international conflict resolution is established. Thus, the strategy of conflict (Schelling, 1960) which has been useful in arms control perhaps may be applicable to interdependent international decisions in the area of population and environment.

No serious attempt has been made to formulate the interdependency of the growth policy of any one nation and global growth policies, but we can identify at least a few specific problems for analysis. In the analysis of conflicts, initial exploration (Choucri, 1972) projects conflicts that could arise from the impacts of growing world population, limited resources, and technological development. Another problem to analyze is that of the uneven distribution of wealth and income among nations. This distribution is an important source of conflict and a motive force behind the interacting global growths of population, economy, and technology. It prods some less-developed countries to emulate the developed countries, often more from psychological needs than from physiological needs of their people. Yet the limits to growth (Meadows et al., 1972) will be reached long before all of the less-developed countries match the material standard of living of the most developed countries. Inasmuch as the need to increase material consumption is psychological, redistribution of wealth is only one way to reduce the conflict. A widespread redefinition of progress, of development, and of quality of life—that is, formulation of new reality and value images—could reduce the conflict and the motivation for growth as well. Some peoples might perceive goals more desirable than of matching the material standard of living of the developed countries. Some less-developed countries could pursue a policy of maximum growth for a limited period of time in order to meet certain lower-level hierarchical needs. At the same time they could prepare themselves for the later pursuit of other goals more consistent with the ecosystem perspective and higher-level hierarchical needs. Furthermore, if the developed countries should adopt a conscious policy of slowing down material growth, or if their attitudes and insti-

tutions should undergo fundamental changes consistent
with ecological order, the growth policies of less-developed countries, having satisfied the physiological needs of
their people, would be correspondingly affected.

To establish common interests does not require that
various countries subscribe to similar value systems, although they might. The emphasis is on threats of mutual
catastrophe and mutual destruction which behoove them
to rise above their conflicting interests. These threats
would be those revealed by studies of the global environmental impact of such things as waste heat, pesticides,
and carbon dioxide, and of the long-term life-supporting
capabilities of Spaceship Earth as a function of global
population and techno-economic growth. The common
interest would be to establish a "new science and new
technology" to serve human needs with allowances for
specific idiosyncrasies in local social and ecological environments.

In a sense, avoidance of catastrophe is a negative
common interest. Other specific areas for research on interdependent international policies could establish positive common interests. For instance, research should encourage mature economic growth into new dimensions.
Information as a commodity has the peculiar characteristic that under certain conditions its value increases when
shared rather than when exclusively possessed. The world
for everyone is more interesting to live in, as well as more
capable of weathering unknown catastrophes, if *diversity*
resulting from the dynamic changes of cultures and life
styles is encouraged. Consequently, the research concerns
are: how to describe meaningfully the sharing and the diversity; to what extent they can be encouraged and by
what values or tradeoff criteria; and what international

policies and institutions must be established, altered, or eliminated to achieve the desired mixtures.

There is no well-established theory for analyzing international strategy and policy in situations where conflict among nations commingles with common interests. Each nation must create its own theory as it analyzes the interdependency between its own national growth policies and global ones. Game theory provides a conceptual lens by which to conjecture about the general nature of the international situation. It is quite likely that a global growth policy decision can be viewed as an "N-person" analogy to the "prisoner's dilemma," a typical example of a non-zero-sum noncooperative game which has a mutually desirable outcome only when the players use a cooperative strategy (Luce and Raiffa, 1957). The "prisoner's dilemma" derives from the problem of two prisoners, separately interrogated, who may confess to a moderate crime in common or accuse each other of a heavy crime; the accuser goes free unless he himself is accused, and the accused receives heavy sentence. Analogously, if all nations base their growth policies on the constraints of the global ecosystem, the ecosystemic integrity is maintained and each nation fares rather well. But, if all adopt maximum growth policies irrespective of ecosystemic impacts, the world becomes unlivable and all nations fare poorly or even perish. This dilemma is accentuated by the fact that the growth policy of a given nation when considered singly may not significantly affect the ecosystem on a global basis. Consequently, regardless of the growths of the other nations, that nation can perceive itself to be better off with a maximum growth policy, assuming its goal is to maximize material consumption. Thus, maximum growth can take precedence over limited growth.

Yet, if each nation were to act rationally in this manner, all would perish. This dilemma can be applied to practically all environmental problems. However, below the international level, government institutions can enter to solve the dilemma.

A global perspective therefore indicates that all nations must cooperate when setting their individual growth policies. Yet cooperation is possible only if no nation is so far behind others in material standards of living that it would consider the status quo worse than a completely despoiled ecosphere. Another condition for such cooperation is that all nations must appreciate this dilemma when considering growth policies and ecosystemic impacts which significantly subordinate their own national interests to the common interests of mankind.

These conditions are difficult enough to meet. In reality the situation is further complicated by certain important aspects which the game theory model does not include. As Rapoport (1966, p. 214) points out, rational analysis "often is at its best when it reveals to us the nature of the situation we find ourselves in, even though it may have nothing to tell us about how we ought to behave in this situation. Too much depends on our choice of values, criteria, notion of what is 'rational'. . . . Game-theoretic analysis, if pursued to its completion, perforce leads us to consider other than strategic modes of thought." Illustrating this point, a recent study of the Cuban crisis (Allison, 1971) shows that historical decisions cannot be explained by considering any national government as a unitary rational actor, a basic assumption in the game theory model. In addition to being a rational game-theoretic move, governmental action in the international scene must be viewed both as an output of intragovernmental organizations and as a resultant of intranational politics. Thus, in any international negotiation related to the macroproblem, it would be very difficult for any government to take the ecosystemic point of view if its organizations have been operating with parochial priorities and short-term perspectives. That is, even government leaders well aware of the "prisoner's dilemma" analogy of the international conflict situation will find it difficult to take a policy stance consistent with the ecosystemic view if political pressures have forced them to commit themselves to the growth ethic.

In light of the present and future policy-making environment in any one nation, one can imagine the magnitude of the task of trying to understand the policy-making processes of some 150 independent nations, each having its own historical, cultural, and ideological background and its own economic position. To this complex web of nations must be added the intranational political structures, and the relations and commitments to various constituencies and social segments in each nation. As one observer caricatured the Stockholm Conference on the Human Environment: "Each delegation consists of an environmental minister, and behind him sits a scientist telling him what to say and a diplomat telling him not to say it" (*Time*, June 19, 1972, p. 55). In sum, game theory provides just an introduction to the tremendous complexity of international negotiations relevant to population and the environment.

Perhaps one cannot be very optimistic about solving the world macroproblem. Nonetheless, there yet is no cause for despair. Just as there are encouraging signs in the United States that future policy-making processes will be more amenable than at present to the comprehensive, synoptic approach, on the worldwide basis there is an increasing likelihood that similar changes will take place.

The world will encounter more and more crises brought about by the macroproblem. Since ecosystemic impacts are local as well as global, those countries most affected locally by their interacting growths of population, economy, and technology are likely to form a coalition and negotiate with other nations.

The formation of coalition, a concept much discussed in "N-person game theory," has characterized recent trends in thinking about the development of common image. This is important. As the basic issue underlying the macroproblem has to do with the challenge to growth and the reality judgment on how growth exerts impact on the ecosystem, *the basic solution to the macroproblem lies in the development of an image shared by the world community.* In a similar fashion the chronological development of balance of power was followed by concepts of collective security and moved toward effective international controls in the area of military conflict. This may presage the development of international cooperation in macroproblem-solving. We can envision the gradual development of a common image through a long and expanding process of functional cooperative activities. For example, several countries may join to monitor air and water pollutants. Their common experience in the project could develop into mutual trust and could attract other countries to the project. They would initiate other joint activities as well. The extended joint activities, and the resulting extended trust, would lead eventually to a common image of global environmental management. Such building of a common image requires fundamental changes in the world views held by many people with different backgrounds. A strategy for stimulating change would begin with "shared margins of items" and proceed toward "shared cores" and eventually "shared matrix of systems" (Pike, 1961).

Another encouraging trend is the exploration of common interests initiated by people in different countries through nongovernmental channels, although final agreements must be authorized by government officials. The Pugwash conferences, for example, were initiated by scientists concerned with the arms race, and contributed significantly to the recent agreement on arms limitation. It is quite likely that initial headway in the macroproblem area will be made by scientists and policy researchers from different countries, working together among themselves and serving to bridge the gap between international projects and parochial projects of policy makers in their respective governments. The Club of Rome has contributed to macroproblem-solving by facilitating the exchange of ideas among scholars and industrialists from many countries. Similar efforts involving different people and different countries can be undertaken and enlarged.

The building of an image shared by the world community will take the time and effort of many people. Toward this end we must encourage each nation in a coalition, and eventually each nation in the world, to adopt a synoptic policy-making process. Policy makers must be encouraged to use the interdisciplinary systems approach in a continuing effort in growth-policy research. Nations then must learn to determine their growth policies in conjunction with other nations on a global ecosystem basis. Only through such international effort can our environmentally compatible common future be secured.

Bibliography of References Cited

Advisory Commission on Intergovernmental Relations. *Urban and Rural America: Policies for Future Growth.* Washington, D.C.: Government Printing Office, 1968. Pp. 186.

Albrecht, William A. "Physical, Chemical and Biochemical Changes in the Soil Community." In *Man's Role in Changing the Face of the Earth,* edited by William L. Thomas. Chicago: University of Chicago Press, 1956. Pp. 648–73.

Alker, Hayward R., Jr. *Mathematics and Politics.* New York: Macmillan Co., 1965. Pp. 152.

Allen, Shirley Walter. *Conserving Natural Resources.* 2d ed. New York: McGraw-Hill Book Co., 1959. Pp. 370.

Allison, Graham T. *Essence of Decision: Explaining the Cuban Missile Crisis.* Boston: Little, Brown, and Co., 1971. Pp. 338.

Argyris, Chris. *Applicability of Organizational Psychology.* New York: Cambridge University Press, 1972. Pp. 138.

————. "The Incompleteness of Social-Psychological Theory: Examples from Small Group Cognitive Consistency and Attribution Research." *American Psychologist,* 24 (October, 1969): 893–908.

————. *Organization and Innovation.* Homewood, Illinois: Richard D. Irwin, 1965. Pp. xii + 274.

"Arid Land Agriculture." *Science,* 171 (March 12, 1971): 989–90.

Ayres, Robert U. "A Materials-Process-Product Model." In *Environmental Quality Analysis,* edited by Allen V. Kneese and Blair T. Bower. Resources for the Future. Baltimore: Johns Hopkins Press, 1972. Pp. 35–68.

Barlow, Robin. *The Economic Effects of Malaria Eradication.* Bureau of Public Health Economics Research Series No. 15. School of Public Health, University of Michigan, Ann Arbor, 1969. Pp. 167.

Bauer, Raymond A., and Gergen, Kenneth J., eds. *The Study of Policy Formation.* New York: Free Press, 1968. Pp. xxii + 392.

Bennis, Warren G. *Changing Organizations.* New York: McGraw-Hill Book Co., 1966. Pp. xi + 223.

Bennis, Warren G., Benne, Kenneth D., and Chin, Robert. *The Planning of Change.* 2d ed. New York: Holt, Rinehart and Winston, 1969. Pp. vii + 627.

Berelson, Bernard. "Beyond Family Planning." *Science,* 163 (February 7, 1969): 533–43.

———, ed. *Family Planning and Population Programs.* Chicago: University of Chicago Press, 1966. Pp. 848.

Berg, Mark R. *Growth, Resources, and Environment.* PROPE Working Paper, 1972. Mimeographed.

Bergman, Ingmar. *The Seventh Seal* (1956). *Four Screenplays of Ingmar Bergman,* translated by Lars Malmstrom and David Kushner. New York: Simon and Schuster, 1960. Pp. 350.

Berry, R. Stephen. "Recycling, Thermodynamics, and Environmental Thrift." *Bulletin of the Atomic Scientists* (May, 1972): 8–15.

Biller, Robert P. "Converting Knowledge into Action: The dilemma and opportunity of the post-industrial society." Paper for panel discussion at Institute for Public Policy Studies, University of California at Berkeley, December 4, 1969. Mimeographed.

Blueprint for Survival. The Ecologist, 2 (January, 1972): 22.

Boulding, Kenneth E. "The Economics of the Coming Spaceship Earth." In *Environmental Quality in a Growing Economy,* edited by Henry Jarrett. Baltimore: Johns Hopkins Press, 1966. Pp. 3–14.

———. *The Image.* Ann Arbor: University of Michigan Press, 1956. Pp. 175.

Brooks, H. "Technology and the Ecological Crisis." Paper presented to the Club of Rome, 1972. Pp. 12. Mimeographed.

Brown, Rex V. "Do Managers Find Decision Theory Useful?" *Harvard Business Review* (May–June, 1970): 78–89.

Buchanan, James M., and Tullock, Gordon. *The Calculus of Consent.* Ann Arbor: University of Michigan Press, 1965. Pp. 361.

Bumpass, Larry, and Westoff, Charles F. "The 'Perfect Contraceptive' Population." *Science,* 169 (September 18, 1970): 1177–82.

Caldwell, Lynton K. "Health and Homeostasis as Social Concepts: An Exploratory Essay." In *Diversity and Stability in Ecological Systems,* edited by G. M. Woodwell and H. H. Smith. Upton, New York: Brookhaven National Laboratory, 1969. Pp. 206–33.

———. *In Defense of Earth: International Protection of the Biosphere.* Bloomington: Indiana University Press, 1972. Pp. 210.

Callahan, Daniel. "Ethics and Population Limitation." *Science,* 175 (February 4, 1972): 487–95.

Chandavarkar, Anand G. "More Growth—More Employment? A Challenge for the Less Developed Countries." *Finance and Development,* 9 (June, 1972): 28–35.

Chen, Kan. "A Macrosystem Analysis of the Human Environment." *Journal of Environmental Systems,* I (June, 1971): 133–52.

———, ed. *Urban Dynamics: Extensions and Reflections.* San Francisco: San Francisco Press, 1972. Pp. 290.

Choucri, Nazli. "Population, Resources, Technology: Political Implications of the Environmental Crises." *International Organization,* 26 (Spring, 1972): 230–60.

Coale, Ansley J. "Man and His Environment." *Science,* 170 (October 9, 1970): 132–36.

Coale, Ansley J., and Hoover, Edgar M. *Population Growth and Economic Development in Low-Income Countries: A Case Study of India's Prospects.* Princeton, New Jersey: Princeton University Press, 1958. Pp. 382.

Coates, Joseph F. "Technology Assessment." *The Futurist* (December, 1971): 225–32.

Commission on Population Growth and the American Future. Report of the Commission. *Population and the American Future.* Washington, D.C.: Government Printing Office, 1972. Pp. 186. Also, New York: New American Library, 1972. Pp. 362. (Page references are to this edition, except when "Report" is denoted.)

Commoner, Barry. *The Closing Circle.* New York: Alfred A. Knopf, 1971. Pp. 326.

Crocker, Thomas D., and Rogers, A. J., III. *Environmental Economics.* Hinsdale, Illinois: Dryden, 1971. Pp. 150.

Daly, Herman E. "Toward a Stationary-State Economy." In *Patient Earth*, edited by John Harte and Robert H. Socolow. New York: Holt, Rinehart and Winston, 1971. Pp. 226–44.

Davies, Gordon W. "The Effect of Immigration on the Canadian Economy." Unpublished Ph.D. dissertation, The University of Michigan, 1972. Pp. 170.

Davis, Kingsley. "The Urbanization of the Human Population," (1965). In *Man and the Ecosphere*, edited by Paul R. Ehrlich, John P. Holdren, and Richard W. Holm. San Francisco: W. H. Freeman and Co. Publishers, 1971. Pp. 267–79.

Day, Lincoln H. "Concerning the Optimum Level of Population." Paper delivered before General Symposium "Is There an Optimum Level of Population?" American Association for the Advancement of Science, Boston, December 30, 1969. Pp. 9.

Dostoevsky, Fyodor. *Winter Notes on Summer Impressions* (1863), translated by Richard Lee Renfeld. New York: McGraw-Hill Book Co., 1965. Pp. 152.

Downs, Anthony. *Inside Bureaucracy*. Boston: Little, Brown, and Co., 1967. Pp. xv + 292.

Dror, Yekezkel. *Public Policymaking Reexamined*. San Francisco: Chandler Publishing Co., 1968. Pp. xiii + 370.

Duncan, Otis Dudley. "Fourteen Observations on Population." Public Hearing Transcript of the Michigan State Special Committee to Study the Impact and Trends of Population Growth in the State of Michigan (October, 1970), pp. 1–10.

Dunn, E. S., Jr. *Economic and Social Development: A Process of Social Learning*. Baltimore: Johns Hopkins Press, 1971. Pp. 327.

Ehrlich, Paul R. "Famine 1975: Fact or Fallacy?" In *The Environmental Crisis*, edited by Harold W. Helfrich, Jr. New Haven and London: Yale University Press, 1970. Pp. 47–64.

———. *The Population Bomb*. Rev. ed. New York: Ballantine Books, 1971. Pp. 201.

———. "The Population Explosion: Facts and Fiction." Zero Population Growth, 1968. Pp. 4.

Ehrlich, Paul R., and Holdren, John P. "Impact of Population Growth." *Science,* 171 (March 26, 1971): 1212–17.

Eisenhower, President Dwight David. "Press Conference, June 9,

1959." *Public Papers of the Presidents of the United States.* Washington, D.C. Pp. 787–88.

Elgin, Duane. "A Conceptual Framework for Population Distribution." Working paper for the Commission on Population Growth and the American Future, 1971. Pp. 7. Mimeographed.

Enke, Stephen. "Economic Consequences of Rapid Population Growth." *The Economic Journal,* 81 (December, 1971): 800–811.

———. "Zero U.S. Population Growth—When, How and Why." General Electric Company, TEMPO Center for Advanced Studies, Report 70TMP-35, Santa Barbara, California, January, 1970. Pp. 22.

Etzioni, Amitai. *The Active Society.* New York: Free Press, 1968. Pp. xxv + 698.

———. "Policy Research." *The American Sociologist.* Supplementary Issue, 6 (June, 1971): 8–12. (A game).

Farvar, M. Taghi, and Milton, John P. eds. *The Careless Technology.* Garden City, New York: Natural History Press, 1972. Pp. 1030.

Feldt, Alan G. "W.A.L.R.U.S. I—Water and Land Resource Utilization Simulation." Environmental Simulation Laboratory, University of Michigan. May, 1972.

Fitch, Lyle C. "National Development and National Policy." In *Environment and Policy: The Next Fifty Years,* edited by William R. Ewald, Jr. Bloomington: Indiana University Press, 1968. Pp. 283–318.

Forrester, Jay W. *World Dynamics.* Cambridge, Mass.: Wright-Allen, 1971. Pp. xiv + 142.

Gamson, William A. *Power and Discontent.* Homewood, Illinois: Dorsey Press, 1968. Pp. xi + 208.

Gillette, Robert. "The Limits to Growth: Hard Sell for a Computer View of Doomsday." *Science,* 175 (March 10, 1972): 1088–92.

Glass, Norman R., and Watt, Kenneth E. F. *Land Use, Energy, Agriculture, and Decison-Making.* A Report to the National Science Foundation, Office of Interdisciplinary Research, Grant No. GI-27, May 28, 1971. Washington, D.C.: National Science Foundation, May 28, 1971. Pp. 235.

Gustafson, David H., et al. "Initial Evaluation of a Subjective

Bayesian Diagnostic System." *Health Services Research* (Fall, 1971): 204–13.

Harary, Frank, Norman, Robert Z., and Cartwright, Dorwin. *Structural Models: An Introduction to the Theory of Directed Graphs*. New York: John Wiley and Sons, 1965. Pp. ix + 415.

Hardin, Garrett. "The Tragedy of the Commons." *Science*, 162 (December 13, 1968): 1243–48.

Harte, John, and Socolow, Robert H. "The Everglades: Wilderness Versus Rampant Land Development in South Florida." In *Patient Earth*, edited by John Harte and Robert H. Socolow. New York: Holt, Rinehart and Winston, 1971. Pp. 181–202.

Havelock, Ronald G. *Innovations in Education: Strategies and Tactics*. Center for Research on Utilization of Scientific Knowledge, Ann Arbor, Michigan: Institute for Social Research, 1971. Pp. 25. Mimeographed.

Havelock, Ronald G., and Guskin, Alan, et al. *Planning for Innovation*. Center for Research on Utilization of Scientific Knowledge, Ann Arbor, Michigan: Institute for Social Research, 1971. Pp. 520.

Heilbroner, Robert L. *The Great Ascent*. New York and London: Harper and Row, Publishers, 1963. Pp. 189.

Heller, Walter H. "Coming to Terms with Growth and the Environment." Paper prepared for the Forum on Energy, Economic Growth, and the Environment, Resources for the Future, Washington, D.C., April 1971. Revised. Pp. 39. Mimeographed; forthcoming in Conference volume.

Helmer, Olaf. *New Developments in Early Forecasting of Public Problems*. Santa Monica, California: RAND, March 1967. Pp. 10.

Hertz, David. "Has Management Science Reached a Dead End?" *Innovation*, 25 (1971): 12–17.

Hoffman, Lois. "The Value of Children to Parents." In *Psychological Prospects on Population*, edited by J. Fawlett. New York: Basic Books, Inc., Publishers, 1973. Pp. 522.

Holmberg, Ingvar. *Fecundity, Fertility, and Family Planning: Application of Demographic Micro Models*. Demographic Institute, University of Gothenburg, Sweden, 1970. Mimeographed.

Horsfall, James G. "The Green Revolution: Agriculture in the Face of the Population Explosion." In *The Environmental Crisis*, edited by Harold W. Helfrich, Jr. New Haven and London: Yale University Press, 1970. Pp. 85–97.

Howard, Ronald A., ed. *Decision Analysis: IEEE Transactions on Systems Science and Cybernetics.* 4 (Special Issue, 1968): 199–366.

Howard, R. A., Matheson, J. E., and North, D. W. "The Decision to Seed Hurricanes." *Science,* 176 (June 16, 1972): 1191–1202.

Institute of Ecology. *Man in the Living Environment.* Report of the Workshop on Global Ecological Problems, 1972. Pp. 265.

Ireland, Thomas. "The Rationale of Revolt." In *Papers on Non-Market Decision Making,* edited by Gordon Tulloch. Charlottesville, Va.: Thomas Jefferson Center for Political Economy, III (Fall, 1967): 49–66.

Jaffe, Frederick S. "Low Income Families: Fertility Changes in the 1960's." *Family Planning Perspectives,* 4 (January, 1972): 43–47.

Janis, Irving L. "Groupthink." *Psychology Today,* 5 (November, 1971): 43–46.

Jones, M. V. "A Technology Assessment Methodology." Report Summary (Project No. 1310) for Office of Science and Technology. The Mitre Corporation, 1971. Pp. 30.

Kahn, Herman. "Alternative World Futures." Paper HI-342-B IV, Hudson Institute, April, 1964.

Keeney, Ralph L. "Utility Functions for Multi-Attribute Consequences." *Management Science,* 18 (January, 1972): 276–87.

Keyfitz, Nathan. *Introduction to the Mathematics of Population.* Reading, Mass.: Addison-Wesley Publishing Co., 1968. Pp. 450.

Knorr, Klaus. "Purposes of an Accelerated Growth Program." In *What Price Economic Growth,* edited by Klaus Knorr and William J. Baumol. *Spectrum.* Englewood Cliffs, New Jersey: Prentice-Hall, 1961. Pp. 1–18.

Kunreuther, Howard. "The Peculiar Economics of Disaster." In *Papers on Non-Market Decision Making,* edited by Gordon Tulloch. Charlottesville, Va.: Thomas Jefferson Center for Political Economy III (Fall, 1967): 67–83.

Kuznets, Simon. *Economic Growth of Nations.* Cambridge, Mass.: Harvard University Press, 1971. Pp. xii + 363.

Lagler, Karl F., ed. *Man-Made Lakes: Planning and Development.* Rome: FAO/UNDP, 1969. Pp. 71.

Lamson, Robert W. "The Future of Man's Environment." *The Science Teacher*, 36 (January, 1969): 25–30.

Leontief, Wassily. "Environmental Repercussions and the Economic Structure: An Input-Output Approach." *The Review of Economics and Statistics*, LII (August, 1970): 262–71.

Leopold, Luna N. "A Procedure for Evaluating Environmental Input." U.S. Geological Circular No. 645, 1971. Pp. 13.

Likert, Rensis. *The Human Organization; Its Management and Values.* New York: McGraw-Hill Book Co., 1967. Pp. ix + 258.

———. *New Patterns in Management.* New York: McGraw-Hill Book Co., 1961. Pp. 279.

Lindblom, Charles Edward. *The Intelligence of Democracy.* New York: Free Press, 1965. Pp. viii + 352.

———. *The Policy-Making Process.* Englewood Cliffs, New Jersey: Prentice-Hall, 1968. Pp. vi + 123.

Lindblom, Charles E., and Hirschman, Albert. "Economic Development, Research and Development, Policy Making: Some Converging Views." *Behavioral Science*, 7 (April, 1962): 211–22.

Looft, William R. "The Psychology of More." *American Psychologist*, 26 (June, 1971): 561–65.

Lucas, J. R. "Moralists and Gamesmen." *Philosophy*, 34 (January, 1959): 1–11.

Luce, Robert D., and Raiffa, Howard. *Games and Decisions.* New York: John Wiley and Sons, 1957. Pp. 509.

Ludlow, John D. *Substantive Results of the University of Michigan's Sea Grant Delphi Inquiry.* Report of the University of Michigan Sea Grant Program (MICHU-SG-72-205). Ann Arbor, Michigan, March 3, 1972. Pp. 115.

Lusted, Lee B. *Introduction to Medical Decision Making.* Springfield, Illinois: Charles C. Thomas, Publisher, 1968. Pp. 271.

March, James G., and Simon, Herbert. *Organizations.* New York: John Wiley and Sons, 1958. Pp. 262.

Marrow, Alfred J., Bowers, David G., and Seashore, Stanley E. *Management by Participation.* New York: Harper and Row Publishers, 1967. Pp. xvi + 264.

Maslow, Abraham H. *Motivation and Personality.* 2d ed. New York: Harper and Row Publishers, 1970. Pp. 369.

Mathes, J. C. "The Henhouse, the Crystal Palace, and the Engineering Curriculum." *Proceedings of the North Central Section of the American Society for Engineering Education,* edited by Helen L. Plants. Pittsburgh, April 16–17, 1971. Pp. 37–41.

Mathes, J. C., and Gray, Donald H. *The Mystique of Technological Progress.* PROPE Working Paper. 1972. Mimeographed.

McHarg, Ian L. "Values, Process and Form." *The Ecological Conscience,* edited by Robert Disch. Englewood Cliffs, New Jersey: Prentice-Hall, 1970. Pp. 21–36.

Meadows, Donella H., Meadows, Dennis L., et al. *The Limits to Growth.* New York: Universe Books, 1972. Pp. 205.

Mesthene, Emanuel G. *Technological Change.* New York: Mentor Press, 1970. Pp. 125.

Meyer, Richard F. "On the Relationship Among the Utility of Assets, the Utility of Consumption and Investment Strategy in an Uncertain but Time-Invariant World." Graduate School of Business Administration, Harvard University, 1969. Pp. 34. Mimeographed.

Michael, Donald. "The Individual: Enriched or Impoverished? Master or Servant?" *Information Technology: Some Critical Implications for Decision Makers.* Report of the Conference Board, New York City, 1972. Pp. 37–60.

———. "On Coping with Complexity: Planning and Politics." In *The Conscience of the City,* edited by Martin Meyerson. New York: George Braziller, 1970. Pp. 89–103. (Also, *Daedalus,* Fall, 1968.)

———. *On the Social Psychology of Learning to Plan—and of Planning to Learn.* Center for Research on the Utilization of Scientific Knowledge, Ann Arbor, Michigan: Institute for Social Research, 1972. Mimeographed; for forthcoming book.

———. *The Unprepared Society: Planning for a Precarious Future.* New York: Basic Books, 1968. Pp. xiv + 132.

Michel, Aloys A. "The Impact of Modern Irrigation Technology on the Indus and Helmand Basins of Southwest Asia." In *The Careless Technology,* edited by M. Taghi Farvar and John P. Milton.

Garden City, New York: Natural History Press, 1972. Pp. 257–75.

Miller, E. J., and Rice, A. K. *Systems of Organization.* London: Tavistock Publications, 1967. Pp. xviii + 286.

Moynahan, Daniel. "Eliteland." *Psychology Today,* 4 (September, 1970): 35–70 ff.

National Academy of Engineering. Committee on Public Engineering Policy. *A Study of Technology Assessment.* Report to the Committee on Science and Astronautics, U.S. House of Representatives, July, 1969. Washington, D.C.: Government Printing Office. Pp. 208.

National Academy of Sciences. *Technology: Process of Assessment and Choice.* Report to the Committee on Science and Astronautics, U.S. House of Representatives, July, 1969. Washington, D.C.: Government Printing Office. Pp. 163.

National Environmental Policy Act of 1969. Public Law 91–190, January 1, 1970. "Appendix A," *Environmental Quality,* the Second Annual Report of the Council on Environmental Quality, August, 1971. Pp. 267–72.

National Science Board. *Environmental Science: Challenge for the Seventies: Summary and Recommendations.* Washington, D.C.: Government Printing Office, 1971. Pp. 55.

National Science Foundation. *Programs for Improving the Dissemination of Scientific Information.* September, 1964. Pp. 18.

Naylor, Thomas H. "Bibliography on Simulation Gaming." *Computer Reviews,* 10 (January, 1969): 61–69.

Nelson, Richard R., Peck, Merton J., and Kalachek, Edward D. *Technology, Economic Growth, and Public Policy.* Washington, D.C.: Brookings Institution, 1967. Pp. xiii + 238.

Oakley, Deborah, and Corsa, Leslie, Jr. *Population Policy for Michigan.* Report for the Population Subcommittee of the Governor's Advisory Council on Environmental Quality, 1971. Pp. 71. Typewritten.

Odum, Eugene P. "The Strategy of Ecosystem Development." *Science,* 164 (April 18, 1969): 262–70.

Odum, Howard T. *Environment, Power and Society.* New York: John Wiley and Sons, 1971. Pp. 331.

Office of Science and Technology. *Electric Power and the Environ-*

ment. Report sponsored by the Energy Policy Staff, Washington, D.C.: Government Printing Office, August, 1970. Pp. xi + 71.

Packer, Arnold, and Moreland, R. Scott. "Two Adaptive Role-Playing Models for Population Planning." Carolina Population Center, Systems Analysis Program, Research Triangle Institute, Research Triangle Park, North Carolina. 1969. Pp. 27.

Pareto, V. *Manuel d'Economie Politique.* 2d ed. Paris: M. Girard, 1927. Pp. 695.

Passell, Peter, Roberts, Marc, and Ross, Leonard. Review of *Limits to Growth,* by D. Meadows et al., and *World Dynamics and Urban Dynamics,* by Jay Forrester. *The New York Times Book Review,* April 2, 1972, pp. 1, 10, 12–13.

Pauly, Mark V. "Bibliography of Recent Works." *Papers on Non-Market Decision Making,* edited by Gordon Tulloch. Charlottesville, Va.: Thomas Jefferson Center for Political Economy, III (Fall, 1967): 105–18.

Peccei, Aurelio. "How to Survive on the Planet Earth." Reprint. *Successo* (February, 1971), pp. 129–38.

Peng, J. Y., Lailybte, Nor, Bakar, A., and Marzuki, Ariffin Bin. "Village Midwives in Malaysia." *Studies in Family Planning,* 2 (February, 1972): 25–27.

Pike, Kenneth L. "Stimulating and Resisting Change." *Practical Anthropology,* 8 (November–December, 1961): 267–74.

Platt, John. "How Men Can Shape Their Futures." *Futures* (March, 1971): 32–47.

———. "What We Must Do." *Science,* 166 (November 28, 1969): 1115–21.

Potter, Robert G. "Additional Births Averted When Abortion Is Added to Contraception." *Studies in Family Planning,* 3 (April, 1972): 53–58.

Price, Don. *The Scientific Estate.* Cambridge, Mass.: Belknap Press, 1965. Pp. 323.

Pugwash Symposium, 1st. *Preventing the Spread of Nuclear Weapons,* edited by C. F. Barnaby. London, 1968. London: Souvenir, 1969. Pp. 374.

———, 10th. *Impact of New Technologies on the Arms Race,* edited by B. T. Feld and others. Racine, Wisconsin, 1970. Cambridge, Mass.: M.I.T. Press, 1971. Pp. 379.

Rapoport, Anatol. *Two-Person Game Theory*. Ann Arbor: University of Michigan Press, 1966. Pp. 229.

Rappaport, Roy A. "Nature, Culture, and Ecological Anthropology." In *Man, Culture and Society*, edited by Harry L. Shapiro. 2d ed. New York and London: Oxford University Press, 1971. Pp. 201–19.

Rehfus, Ruth. *Barriers to Decision Making Information*. PROPE Working Paper, 1972. Pp. 21. Mimeographed.

Rein, Martin. "Social Policy Analysis as the Interpretation of Beliefs." *American Institute of Planners Journal*, 37 (September, 1971): 277–310.

Ridker, Ronald G. "Population and Pollution in the United States." *Science*, 176 (June 9, 1972): 1085–90.

Rogers, Everett, and Shoemaker, F. Floyd. *Communication of Innovations*. New York: Free Press, 1971. Pp. xix + 476.

Rose, Sanford. "The Economics of Environmental Quality." *Fortune*, 91 (February, 1970): 120 ff.

Rosenthal, Robert, and Weiss, Robert. "Problems of Organizational Feedback Processes." In *Social Indicators*, edited by Raymond A. Bauer. Cambridge, Mass.: M.I.T. Press, 1966. Pp. 302–41.

Rotter, Julian B. "Generalized Expectancies for Interpersonal Trust." *American Psychologist*, 26 (May, 1971): 443–52.

Russell, Clifford S., and Landsberg, Hans H. "International Environmental Problems—A Taxonomy." *Science*, 172 (June 25, 1971): 1307–14.

Samuelson, Paul A. *Economics*. New York: McGraw-Hill Book Co., 1961. Pp. 853.

Schelling, Thomas C. *The Strategy of Conflict*. London and New York: Oxford University Press, 1960. Pp. 309.

Schick, Allen. "System Politics and Systems Budgeting." *Public Administration Review*, 29 (March–April, 1969): 137–51.

Schon, Donald A. *Technology and Change*. New York: Delacorte Press, 1967. Pp. xix + 248.

Schultz, T. Paul. "An Economic Model of Family Planning and Fertility." *Journal of Political Economy*, 77 (March–April, 1969): 153–80.

Schuphan, W. "Nitrate Problems and Nitrate Hazards as Influenced by Ecological Conditions and by Fertilization of Plants." In *The Careless Technology*, edited by M. Taghi Farvar and John P. Milton. Garden City, New York: Natural History Press, 1972. Pp. 577–90.

Schwartz, Eugene S. *Overskill*. Chicago: Quadrangle Books, 1971. Pp. 338.

Shubik, Martin. "Modeling on a Grand Scale." Review of *World Dynamics*, by Jay Forrester. *Science*, 174 (December 3, 1971): 1014–15.

Skolimowski, Henryk. "Technology: The Myth Behind the Reality." *Architecture Association Quarterly* (London), (July, 1970): 21–31.

Slichter, Sumner H. *Economic Growth in the United States*. New York: Free Press, 1961. Pp. 189.

Solo, Robert A. "New Maths and Old Sterilities." *Saturday Review* (January 22, 1972): 47–48.

Stanford Research Institute. *Master Social Indicators*. Menlo Park, California: Stanford Research Institute, 1969. Pp. 52.

Stead, Frank M. "Desalting California." *Environment*, 11 (June, 1969): 2–10.

Study of Critical Environmental Problems. Report of the Study. *Man's Impact on the Global Environment*. Cambridge, Mass.: M.I.T. Press, 1970. Pp. 319. (SCEP Report).

Theobald, Robert, ed. *Social Policies for America in the Seventies: Nine Divergent Views*. Garden City, New York: Doubleday, 1968. Pp. 216.

Thompson, Wilbur. *A Preface to Urban Economics*. Resources for the Future. Baltimore: Johns Hopkins Press, 1965. Pp. 413.

"World News," *Time*, June 19, 1972, p. 55.

Tsongas, G. A., et al. "A Means of Radiation of Earth Thermal Pollution." *Proceedings: Energy 70*. Fifth Intersociety Energy Conversion Engineering Conference, Las Vegas, Nevada, September, 1970. Pp. 20.

Turvey, Ralph. "Side Effects of Resource Use." In *Environmental Quality in a Growing Economy*, edited by Henry Jarrett. Baltimore: Johns Hopkins Press, 1966. Pp. 55–71.

U.S. Senate. Committee on Interior and Insular Affairs. *Selected Readings on Economic Growth*. 2 parts. Washington, D.C.: Government Printing Office, September, 1971. Pp. ix + 678.

Vickers, Sir Geoffrey. *The Art of Judgment*. London: Methuen, 1965. Pp. 242.

——. *Freedom in a Rocking Boat*. New York: Basic Books, 1971. Pp. 215.

Von Neumann, John, and Morgenstern, Oskar. *Theory of Games and Economic Behavior*. New York: John Wiley and Sons, 1964. Pp. 641.

Warwick, Donald. "Socialization and Personality." In *Management of Urban Crisis*, edited by Stanley Seashore and Robert McNeill. New York: Free Press, 1971. Pp. 378–414.

Webb, Eugene J. "Individual and Organizational Forces Influencing the Interpretation of Indicators." Institute for Defense Analysis research paper (P-488), Washington, D.C., April, 1969. Pp. 45. Mimeographed.

White, Gilbert F., Lagler, Karl F., et al. *Man-Made Lakes as Modified Ecosystems*. SCOPE Report No. 2. Rome: International Council of Scientific Unions, 1972. Pp. 75.

White, Leslie W. "The Historical Roots of Our Ecological Crisis." *Science*, 155 (March 10, 1967): 1203–7.

Wicker, Tom. "U.S. Needs a Cure for Income Inequities," *Detroit Free Press*. July 3, 1972.

Wildavsky, Aaron B. *Politics of the Budgetary Process*. Boston: Little, Brown and Company, 1964. Pp. xi + 216.

Wilensky, Harold L. *Organizational Intelligence*. New York: Basic Books, 1967. Pp. 226.

Wolman, Abel. "The Metabolism of Cities." *Scientific American*, 213 (September, 1965): 178–94.

Young, Jeffrey W., Arnold, William F. III, and Brewer, John W. "Parameter Identification and Dynamic Models of Socio-Economic Phenomena." Department of Mechanical Engineering, University of California, Davis, 1972. Pp. 29. Mimeographed.

About the Authors

MARK R. BERG is currently a doctoral student in urban and regional planning at the University of Michigan. Mr. Berg is a member of the steering committee of the New Science Group, and was a research associate with Project PROPE.

E. DRANNON BUSKIRK is presently a teaching fellow and doctoral student in resource development in the School of Natural Resources at the University of Michigan, with a particular interest in water quality. Mr. Buskirk was a research associate with project PROPE.

KAN CHEN is Paul G. Goebel Professor of Advanced Technology and professor of electrical and computer engineering at the University of Michigan. Previously, he was professor of environmental systems engineering at the University of Pittsburgh, director of the Institute-wide Program on Urban Development at Stanford Research Institute, and manager, Systems Technology Research and Development at Westinghouse Electric Corporation, Pittsburgh. Dr. Chen is currently president for technical activities of the IEEE Systems, Man and Cybernetics Society.

DONALD H. GRAY is associate professor of civil engineering at the University of Michigan. Dr. Gray has been acting director of the Institute for Environmental Quality at the university. He teaches an interdisciplinary course on the assessment of environmental impact of technological projects. He is active in the American Society of Civil Engineers, and chairman of the Committee on Environmental Concerns in Geotechnical Engineering.

KARL HERPOLSHEIMER is a graduate student in economics and finance at the University of Michigan. Mr. Herpolsheimer was a research associate with Project PROPE.

T. JEFFREY JONES is a graduate student in the Program for Engineering for Public Systems at the University of Michigan. He was a research associate with Project PROPE.

GEORGE KRAL is a graduate student in urban planning at the University of Michigan. Mr. Kral was a research associate with Project PROPE.

KARL F. LAGLER is professor of natural resources in the School of Natural Resources and professor of zoology in the College of Literature, Science, and the Arts at the University of Michigan. Dr. Lagler has published extensively in the field of aquatic resource ecology and has been a USOM adviser at Kasetstart University, Thailand, and coordinator of multidisciplinary Lake Resource Development Projects in Africa at FAO, Rome. Since 1968, Professor Lagler has been a senior consultant to FAO and UNDP, and an adviser to WHO and, beginning in 1970, to the Mekong Committee of UN/ECAFE. He is a director of Resource Development Associates, fellow of AAAS and diplomat of the French Academy of Agriculture.

J. C. MATHES is associate professor of humanities, College of Engineering, at the University of Michigan. Dr. Mathes is chairman of the Undergraduate Interdisciplinary Engineering Program, and is a member of the steering committee of the New Science Group. Dr. Mathes is a member of the American Society for Engineering Education, the Society for Technical Communication, the Midwest Modern Language Association, and the IEEE Systems, Man and Cybernetics Society.

JOHN McGUIRE is assistant professor of biostatistics and population planning in the School of Public Health at the University of Michigan.

DONALD N. MICHAEL is professor of planning and public policy, professor of psychology, and program director for the Center for Research on Utilization of Scientific Knowledge, Institute for Social Research, at the University of Michigan. Dr. Michael has had extensive professional experience in government agencies, private organizations, with professional journals, and at universities.

STEPHEN M. POLLOCK is associate professor of industrial and operations engineering at the University of Michigan, and director of the Graduate Program in Engineering for Public Systems. Dr. Pollock has held professorial rankings in the Department of Operations Analysis of the Naval Postgraduate School, and has been employed as an operations analyst and consultant by Arthur D. Little, Inc., Cambridge, Massachusetts. Dr. Pollock is active in the Operations Research Society of America and is associate editor, *SIAM Journal of Applied Mathematics*.

RUTH REHFUS is a library scientist and has been a scholar in conservation at the School of Natural Resources of the University of Michigan. Ms. Rehfus has held positions with the Cleveland Public Library, the San Diego City Schools Library, the U.S. Department of the Interior Library, and with the Great Lakes Fishery Laboratory Library in Ann Arbor. Ms. Rehfus was a research associate with Project PROPE.

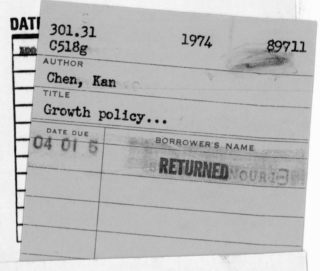